Allow Them the
Opportunity to Change

(An Effective Guide for Mentoring
"Troubled" Youth)

By Sidney W. Johnson

*"Mentoring is to support and encourage people to manage **their** own learning in order that they may maximize **their** potential, develop **their** skills, improve **their** performance and become the person **they** want to be."*

Eric Parsloe

This is a Change Is Possible Publishing Book

Dedication

This book is dedicated to the millions of young people around the world who have developed feelings of hopelessness. There have been times over the years my own hope has dimmed. As a child, I was very poor, often undervalued, and did not receive the kind of nurturing a child needs to grow up feeling confident and self-assured. As a result I struggled with self-esteem on the inside while appearing strong and confident on the outside. This lack of self-confidence filled me with fear, and caused me to isolate myself into small circles that hindered my growth and limited my opportunities.

I was bullied as a young boy by those who were supposed to be my friends. In response to being bullied, I became a bully. I picked out weaker kids and transferred my feelings of worthlessness on to them, and then laughed on the outside, while living in guilt, shame, and remorse on the inside over the pain I had caused. I became self-abusive. I lived spontaneously, even when it became clear that doing so was hurting me. I lacked self-control and blamed everyone for my failures. I did not meet my biological father until I was 25 years old. I was nearly 40 years old when I heard my mother tell me she loved me for the first time. I did not know how to show love or receive love. When love came to me, I pushed it away as attempts to change me, and hung on to false pride. My self-esteem had been so damaged that almost instinctively my life purpose became to impress others in order to gain their acceptance.

However, no matter how much acceptance I gained from others, self-acceptance continued to be my major problem. So, even when success came, I continued to be plagued by my internal issues causing me to sabotage myself and blame others when things went wrong.

I dedicate this book to you because in you I see myself, and my prayer is that this book fills those who work with you with knowledge, patience and wisdom that builds their tolerance and allows them to penetrate the walls of defense you have put up, and persevere through the outbursts that some of you will surely have, until they have gained your trust. Then, once they have gained your trust, you allow them to help you. Consequently, you will not have to waste years of your lives, getting in your own way, but your hope can be restored, and you can actually begin to live the lives you were born to live.

Allow Them

the Opportunity to Change

Table of Contents

Acknowledgments

I must start by giving all praise and honor to God whose favor in my life has never wavered, and whose grace and mercy have sustained me through many mistakes and growing pains. Thank you for creating me for a purpose. Thank you for the pain, trials, and tribulations I experienced growing up for those experiences have shaped me into the man I am today. Because of the pain I have experienced, I can identify with the pain in others, and in that identification I have been blessed to help many. With your continued favor, I can continue to help many more.

Tina Sanders, thank you for believing in me and always supporting my ideas. Your belief, guidance, and support allowed me the freedom to be myself, and it is no accident that while under your leadership my programs touched the lives of a lot of young people.

Faye Sigers, thank you for opening my mind to the possibilities the world held for me, and giving me the encouragement to shun traditional wisdom and follow my dreams. You have been my angel, and I am forever grateful to God for bringing you into my life.

Dr. Sudiata Djata, thank you for the many history lessons you provided, both in and out of the classroom. They prepared me for the world, and helped me find my place in the struggle.

Thank you to my technical support team Cydni C. Polk, LaTrice Davis, Eddie White, and Christy Toney. Thank you all for the editorial, graphic, and technical assistance you provided in helping me bring my ideas to life. I could not have finished without you.

Thank you to all of my former staff for allowing your skills to create quality programs in support of my visions. Together we advised, cried, laughed, shared successes, suffered setbacks, and argued with our students together, and as a result we often took the job home together. Yet together we built wonderful programs that touched the lives of a lot of children.

Thank you to all of the principals, counselors, teachers, administrators, janitors, office workers, and support staff of the various schools that have housed my programs over the years. I know first-hand the challenges you face in your efforts to educate our young people, many of whom face a host of undiagnosed mental issues, and often with budget restrictions and limited resources. Thank you for the work you do on a daily basis, and for the access and support you have given me and my staff over the years.

Thank you to all of the parents who have allowed me to work with your children over the years. You have made the last 17 years of my life most rewarding, and I pray that my presence in your lives and the lives of your children has touched your lives as much as you have touched mine.

Finally, thank you to my own family. My children, Dmari, Jordan, and Sydney, thank you for always making me feel like the greatest dad in the world. When one chooses a career of service, the family is forced to share their loved one with strangers. You all have handled my absences with grace and elegance. You have befriended the students who were important to me and welcomed them into our family. I love you more than words can express. My wonderful wife Sonya, you have been my biggest cheerleader and made tremendous personal sacrifices to your own dreams in order to support mine over the years. This book would not have been possible without you, and I am eternally grateful.

Preface

I first found a passion for working with youth when I was a student at Northern Illinois University. I was hired as a teacher/mentor for a program called Upward Bound, which focused on helping low income and first generation college students get into college. I realized early on when working with these students that many of them were in pain and more than tutoring, needed caring adults with whom they could talk freely without fear of judgment. I discovered a passion for being that caring adult. I found a home with Boys & Girls Clubs, where I received the training to go with the passion, allowing me to touch the lives of many children over the years.

In February 2010 I received a call from Tina Sanders, a former supervisor from my days with Boys & Girls Clubs of Chicago. Tina called to ask me if I had any ideas about what could be done to stop the endless wave of violence that seemed to be taking over the city of Chicago. The wave of violence was so out of control that it was decimating the ranks of potentially strong leaders who otherwise might emerge from among our youth. Tina had decided that she wanted to establish a mentoring program to do something to address this crisis. She called me to see if I would be interested in helping her develop the program, and also to stay and facilitate.

Ironically, Tina's call came on the heels of the death of Derrion Albert. Derrion Albert was a young man who attended Christian Fenger High School on the south side of Chicago. Derrion was killed as a result of a vicious beating that he took at the hands of several young men during a massive brawl outside his school. The fight was caught on video tape and within minutes had gone viral. Despite the realities that: the fight occurred outside the school; was between warring neighborhoods; and was not directly the blame of anyone at the school; Chicago Public Schools, the city of Chicago, and Chicago residents in general were embarrassed by this video. The collective thought around town was that something had to be done to show that Chicagoans were sympathetic to the challenges faced by some of our most at risk students. The idea among social service providers was that programs needed to be developed that could create calmer school environments and provide additional support for the children who were most at risk for being victims or perpetrators of violence.

The idea could not have come at a better time with so many children in Chicago, and around the nation being victims of violence. Unfortunately, Derrion Albert was just one in a long line of children killed. In fact, things had gotten so bad by 2010 that Education Secretary Arne Duncan when discussing the violence in Chicago stated that he was haunted by it, "we don't live in Iraq" he commented. (Chicago Sun-Times 9/22/2010). Mr. Duncan's comments were insightful, as Carol Marin of the Chicago Sun-Times reported in March of 2010 that 20 Chicago Public School students had been killed in the 8 months since school started in comparison with only 16 Chicago soldiers who were killed over the period of 7 years in Iraq and Afghanistan. (Chicago Sun-Times 3/21/2010). While the numbers reported by the Sun-Times were startling to some, the reality is that the residents of Chicago's south and west sides were not at all surprised. Most had long ago become desensitized to the violence until it directly affected them, while others battled feelings of powerlessness when it came to battling the violence. There was plenty of blame being tossed around. Some blamed the government, some blamed the schools, and others blamed the parents. Meanwhile while people looked around to find somewhere to place the blame, an entire generation of young people was being decimated. To say I was troubled by all of this would be an understatement. I was deeply grieved and tormented by it. I had been working with young people for over 15 years, and in the past 3 years, I had lost 3 times as many children as I had in the first 12 years combined.

So, although I had never worked with Derrion Albert personally, I was moved to tears over his death. I am always moved and troubled when a child gets hurt or killed. I recognize the value in the life that was lost, the potential that was carried in that life, and the beauty the world will miss as a result of that life being taken prematurely. I also see the missed potential in the alleged assailants in such cases, as this too usually involves the pre-mature destruction of young lives, often turned over to the prison industrial complex, many of them to be faced with worse fates than their victims. However, as emotional as I normally get when a child is killed, I was twice as emotional when Derrion Albert was killed. Maybe it was the brutal nature in which he died; maybe it was the fact that it was caught on videotape and constantly replayed; or maybe it was the combination of his death and the correlation between it and all of the other children who had been the victims of violence that became too much for me to bear. Whatever it was, I just knew that I had enough. I knew I could not sit around in my cushy office and say I was a Youth Development Professional, while kids were dying, and yet not get involved in the efforts to keep them safe.

So, the night Derrion Albert was killed, I was moved to the point of tears. I cried, not regular tears, but an abundance of tears. However, I knew I could not rest with just the tears. I wanted to do something, but I was not sure what. That night, I took out a pen and began to write what I thought could be done to address the problem. I knew we could not change the environment in which these children lived without an extraordinary amount of money and resources that I surely did not have. So, I figured we had to change the children. I knew in order to change the children we had to shun traditional theories and be willing to allow the children to get to know us on a real level. We had to stop judging them; we had to stop being self-righteous ourselves; we had to acknowledge their present reality; and we had to start to have real dialogue with them.

We had to open the door for transparency, and in that transparency would lay the path to their freedom. That was what I wrote on that night…and the next day, Tina Sanders called me.

When I spoke to Tina and she told me that she thought about me when she had the idea of developing a mentoring program, I felt like it was divine intervention. I believed that a door was being opened for me to not only help several students, but to introduce a new way of looking at the behavioral problems of an entire generation of misunderstood young people, whom we call troubled. The educational system and social structures currently in place for our young people was clearly failing them. They were failing them, not intentionally as I had once suspected. But, they were failing them because they were ignoring the reality that until children are loved, socialized, and accepted for who they are, they will be difficult to formally educate. Until educators, and social workers begin to take a holistic approach to education, factoring in a child's loving environment, and his living environment as well as his learning environment, too many of our children would be allowed to go through the system (No Child Left Behind) while lacking the basic life skills it would take to ensure any long term success. This is not just true for inner cities, or areas of high poverty, as evident by random shootings in Colorado, Oregon, Wisconsin, Connecticut, and a growing list of other places. Many of the assailants in mass shootings of this nature on the surface come from good homes and good schools, leaving those who know them stunned.   Yet, after closer examinations are conducted, the individuals who commit these atrocities are much more "troubled" than anyone ever suspected. Somewhere along the way the individuals who commit these tragedies no longer felt the love and security they needed to make it in the world. How different could the outcome had been, had these individuals had mentors who could have helped identify their issues, and then stayed to help navigate through the issues they had identified? Systemic breakdowns often allow early indicators to be missed, causing "troubled" youth to miss the help they need. This fact, combined with children being labeled as "troubled" after minor incidents that could just as easily be classified as youthful exuberance, create a self-fulfilling prophecy of "trouble" for many young people.

It is easy to point fingers as to why these breakdowns occur, but finger pointing always proves divisive and does little to address the issues at hand. The bottom line is: teachers are paid to teach; principals are paid to run schools; and guidance counselors are paid to see that students are equipped with the information they need to ensure they meet graduation requirements, and when possible, apply and meet college admission requirements. Who gets paid to fill in the gaps? When parents are unavailable during crucial after-school hours where do children go to get the love, nurturing, advice, advocacy, and support they need to grow up healthy and confident?

These were the questions I asked myself, and I knew that if we hoped to survive this current trend of violence and failure that has dominated our country in recent years, we had better answer these questions fast and someone had better step up and assume these responsibilities.

We found evidence of students with severe academic deficiencies as we began to mentor children in Chicago. We tested students who were in the 10th, $11^{th,}$ and 12th grades and found that many were reading and writing on 2nd and 3rd grade levels. The sad part was that among the high risk students we tested the low performing students were not the exception, but the norm. However, in spite of their low test scores we found many of the students to be extremely intelligent, yet lacking basic skills. When we had students to test on 7th and 8th grade levels, they were among the higher functioning population of students tested. Many of the students we tested were as expected, also among the most truant students in school, as well as among those who presented the most behavioral challenges in school.

In spite of their controversial history, we approached these students with open minds and hearts and found that this approach allowed us to quickly gain their trust, and acceptance as authentic. This authenticity became the cornerstone of our mentoring program. It allowed the students to view us differently than many of the other adults who had come into their lives. This level of trust and acceptance created relationships in which students were willing to share their stories with us, freeing us to address issues with them that were at the core of their problems in school, home, and life, and opening up help for them that was previously unavailable. This guide will share some of those stories in an effort to create an understanding of the depths of the issues facing this generation of young people, as well as the access to resources that will be necessary if they are to *truly* be helped. This guide is intended specifically for parents, teachers, counselors, politicians, religious leaders, social workers, concerned citizens, and all those who come in contact with children who are "troubled", and deal with the frustration of feeling their efforts to help these children are in vain. The lack of progress we see in our children often creates a frustration that at its core is rooted in a seemingly inability to help children who want to be helped. This book will provide some answers and relief to that frustration.

Foreword

MENTORING, AN ANSWER

(Taking a gallant stance in the Gap)

By Ken Harris

Evolution of the Role of Mentoring

The role of mentoring has evolved over the years. Over the past 60 years or so, the role of mentor was primarily as an advisor and could be served by almost anyone, a brother, aunt, neighbor, teacher, or supervisor. During that time, and in most cases, the role of mentor was held by someone with whom the mentee had already established a congenial or intimate relationship. Then, about 40 years ago, the term took on more formalized roots with companies assigning more experienced employees to mentor entry level and rising employees to help maximize their potential. About 25 years ago the role of professional mentor emerged as the workforce, social service and educational arenas began to recognize the need to use coaches or mentors to help employees, clients and students respectively, to help assist them with deficiencies in their performance or development.

Most of these mentors had clearly defined limits, duties and responsibilities. They had contracts with start and end dates. Some were required to carry phones and to be available after regular work hours. In most cases, the role of mentor was a business relationship with some tenements of a personal relationship. However, as time passed the gap widened between the emerging societal expectations of what was required by human capitol vs. what emerging youth and young adults were able to provide and deliver, and as a result the role of mentor became institutionalized. The role now enjoys the status of being one of many critical roles identified in helping to maximize human capitol.

Though the role is in the same cluster, it is not synonymous with teachers, case managers, parole officers, and counselors. Instead it tends to linger somewhere behind these when it comes to sustaining the role through funding challenges and in establishing a hierarchy or pecking order among these various roles. This is true even though, in many cases, the role of mentor overlaps each of these areas, and for its most needy mentees, could include some tenements of a parenting role as well.

This new role assumes a more strategic approach to mentoring. It takes into account certain factors that are undeniably a catalyst that calls for mentoring on a more in depth basis with more heavily involved interventions. It takes on additional character and depth and tends to be more far reaching. Its evolution, by necessity, fills multiple needs for the mentee, but can also include meeting the needs of significant others close to the mentee, as well.

Evolution of the Expanded Need of the Role

The following is written not to give excruciating detail or a concise chronological history that explains the dilemma we face with regard to the plight facing our children. It instead is a general accounting of events and emerging trends that lend a perspective as to how we might explain our current crisis situation with youth, while simultaneously pointing to some vital recovery measures that are necessary to move our children out of the doldrums of this dilemma.

In pursuing this discourse, we will primarily focus upon the African –American experience in America in stating our case, not because it represents any mutual exclusivity to the problem at hand, but instead, because it represents a plausible representation of how a series of events might have led to our present demise and also lends itself to a much read about, studied, and documented sample of how we arrived at this crisis. And, to reiterate, it should be noted that this crisis is by no means mutually exclusive to the African-American. All races, at different and variant levels face the same dilemma and require mentoring as one of the same key remedies.

Even today, America remains ripe with the memory of the term community or "village", which is a word that emanated from many parts of Africa and took roots in America to help explain how African-Americans worked together as a collective to survive the plight of slavery, post-slavery, and child raising with vision and purpose. Thus we get the phrase, "It takes a 'village' to raise a child." So, this African expression of community became a mantra in America within and among African-American populations in the U. S. during slavery, post slavery and agricultural periods, and on through the industrial periods.

In the 1950's children in the "village" were raised conservatively and were taught to mimic mainstream America, usually on a shoestring budget. Their lives were primarily spent in the neighborhoods where they were born. Children were raised "to be seen, but not heard". This basically meant that children were to: stay in "their place", act and behave like children, and stay out of grown folks business. Children had clearly defined roles; they were to be modest, respectful, and to always conduct themselves first and foremost as children. They were to be conservatively dressed, with boys wearing khaki pants and jerseys or oxford shirts and hush puppy shoes. Girls wore white blouses, A-line, navy blue skirts, bobby sox and plain shoes, with the few dress style exceptions clearly defined. Girls were told, "Keep your hemlines down below your knees and your legs crossed, so that nothing gets in, and definitely no make-up." Anything outside of this "norm" was considered to be for the most part, exclusive to entertainers, and performers. Anyone found darning "loud" colors, bright colors, and mixing plaids with stripes, and/or polka dots would be considered, flamboyant, gaudy or risqué and would possibly face the risk of being marginalized. Meals were prepared at home each day. Trips to McDonald's were a special and infrequent treat. Family structures were tight. Communities were tight. Everybody looked out for everybody else and if any nonsense took place in that community, it was revealed, and addressed. The morals of that time were much simpler than today.

This term "The Village" became especially pungent again during the 60s and 70s, when African-Americans emerged as a prolific force to be reckoned with. This was during a time of rapid self-discovery, self-identity, self-appreciation and self-actualization for many African-Americans. In the sixties, a new cultural order emerged. The African-American community began to redefine itself through the lens of pride. Collectively, they tired of discrimination and racism. Protests, marches, and demonstrations against discrimination became the order of the day. Swept up in this wave of pride were children.

In the seventies, this trend continued as African-Americans began to define for themselves what beauty looked like rather than to have it defined for them. Braids, dread locks, naturals, dashikis, jeans, sandals, and natural looks came to personify the new vision of beauty and pride for the African-American. This transformation occurred while the various other revolutions were taking place in mainstream America: free love, anywhere and everywhere (Woodstock), Hard Rock and Rap, and Anti-war demonstrations (Viet Nam).

During this time of transformation, treating those diagnosed with light to heavy mental illnesses became less of a priority. In a documentary called "The Killing Floor" the issue was explored that spoke to the federal government testing drugs on certain populations in the communities, including street hustlers, children of the night, prisoners, alcoholics, and those with diagnosed mental illness. Add to the equation, the casual and recreational use of drugs that led to full blown addictions, as well as sexual confusion with women in pants and short haircuts, and men wearing pink, carrying purses, and jewelry while in high heeled shoes, a new sub-culture slowly emerged as a semi-accepted mainstreamed way of life. The issues brought about by this new sub-culture led to single parent families, girls wearing wigs, weaves, and adult fashions, including miniskirts (Twiggy), daisy dukes, and higher hemlines. The community was affected by no curfews being enforced, both parents working, single parent homes, young teens becoming parents, food additives making girls shapelier even as little girls, leading to younger girls with older guys. Advancements in technology eliminated many jobs that required only a high school education, and more and more companies moved overseas to avoid high labor costs in America creating a state of dis-ease among the disenfranchised in America. This state of dis-ease is where we find America today, and is the primary reason why mentoring has to become a funding priority if America and her children are to survive.

Change is Hard for Me

As a child I had ambition,

But they told me my competition was superior…

So my ambition went missing.

Now, I'm the monster that you envisioned I'd be.

But the reality is, you created this guy.

Placed guns around me and told me I'd die.

So, now I'm just living the life I was destined to live.

The streets showed me love, they got Us as kids.

Then they want me to change at the age of 17,

But what makes you think you can really reach me?

I'm cursed, I'm hurt!

My self-esteem is so low that my heaven is…dirt.

So, if you want to reach me, sell me a dream…

Tell me I can change the world and do great things.

Go ahead, because deep down I know in me there is good

…but the pain of my hood reminds me I am no good.

Maybe one day I will change,

…but for now I think things will stay the same.

Until I can be accepted for me…the real me,

But first I must find me…the real me.

Who is going to help me with that?

By D'mari M. Johnson

Chapter One

<u>The Problem</u>

What's Wrong with Today's Youth?

"When someone was hitting me, or like sexually molesting me, it just seemed normal to continue to do those things to myself". **Tatum O'Neal**

With today's generation of young people, there exists a disconnect between them and their predecessors that makes it extremely difficult to gain any progress with the young people, leaving them the first generation in ages to probably face more difficult lives than their parents faced. A large part of the reason for this disconnect comes from the reality that adults are finding it increasingly difficult to work with young people, and children are becoming increasingly distrustful of adults. Adults from my generation love to reminisce about the good old days when life was simple. Back in the days when we: respected our elders, went to church on Sunday, did our homework before playing afterschool, played peacefully with our friends, did our chores, and were overall just positive kids. What happened to those days? When I hear these comments, I cannot help but think I do not know that they ever existed.

It is "not my problem"

Seriously, one cannot argue against the seemingly vast differences between children who grew up in the 70's and children growing up today. However, one of my pet peeves is when someone randomly asks the question, "What's wrong with these kids today?" My response is usually something like a better question is, "what's wrong with the adults who are raising them?" Often times, children get blamed because adults simply find it easier to question and treat the symptoms, rather than deal with the real issues. Adults often forget the difficulty of growing up, especially in inner cities and areas high in poverty. During one of my workshops I attempt to describe what is going on in the mind of a young person whom we consider to be "troubled" and at risk. To best describe what one is facing in these environments I use an example I borrowed from Bishop T.D. Jakes. I saw Bishop Jakes do this exercise during one of his sermons and it stuck with me.

Statistics say that one in every third girl and one in every fifth boy has probably been molested by someone whom the family trusts. The molesters range from babysitters, to cousins and distant relatives, to step parents, to even siblings. The one element that the molesters share in common is that they have a sense of comfort that allows them to feel that they can not only do the unthinkable, but they can get away with it. During this activity I walk thru the audience and ask every third woman and every fifth man to stand. I ask everyone else to look around the room, and I tell them that chances are, according to statistics that these people have been molested. It is something about this activity that drives the point home of the damage being done through these molestations. Whenever I use this activity, I can look around the room at the faces of the people who are standing, and I can almost tell the ones who have been molested. I have had people break down and cry; I have had people approach me after the training to talk about their abusers; and I even had a woman run out of a session sobbing. Just from thinking about abuse that happened years ago, many adults experience emotional breakdowns; and are unwilling or unable to even talk about the abuse. So, my point in the training is that if adults, who are educated have a difficult time recovering from such traumatic events to the point that they cannot publicly discuss their experiences, then what is to be expected of children who suffer from these tragedies, and oftentimes are still living in the same environments where the tragedies have occurred?

The other fact that must be considered when relating this concept to children with whom you may come in contact is that molestation only covers one form of abuse. When these children's situations are studied closely, one will find a host of traumatic experiences causing emotional breakdowns for those young people who have experienced them. In other words, sexual abuse is still only one form of abuse. There is also mental and emotional abuse, physical abuse, psychological abuse, and even neglect. Each of the various types of abuse is deadly in its own way, and each brings with it a host of problems that its victims will have to overcome. Although the causes of abuse can range from any number of things, poverty is right there at the top of the list. According to a report by CBS News released in 2009, reports of child abuse increased during the recent economic recession, directly implying a connection between poverty and abuse. Therefore, mentors and teachers who work in areas and during times where poverty levels are high should be trained not only in recognizing signs of abuse, but steps that should be taken when abuse is suspected. In Illinois, for example anyone who works with children from the ages of day care through high school is required to take an annual training on the Illinois Department of Children and Family services website on being a Mandated Reporter. This is a good place to start for anyone who suspects abuse.

In addition to the possibility of abuse, there are other problems that make reaching today's youth difficult. Not the least of which is the difference between adults in the 1970's and the adults of today. Part of the reason we were able to do things like roam the neighborhood unattended, stay out until the street lights came on, and just enjoy our youth more back then was because the adults were the adults. One major lesson I learned in my years of providing direct service to youth, which I will continue to repeat is that children in any area are looking for primarily structure and consistency from the adults in their lives. Structure makes children feel safe, and consistency makes children believe they are being treated fairly. When these components are in place, children are typically happy, productive, and easy to work with.

This brings us back to the question of today's youth and what is wrong with them. The problem for many of today's youth is that the adults in their lives are failing to provide them with the tools they need to be successful. I am not referring to just the parents when I say this. The biggest difference I see in the adults of today versus the adults of my youth is the lack of involvement and commitment by the adults of today. When I was a child, the adults in the community, schools, parks, and churches took more than a passing interest in our behavior, and they called us on it when our behavior was inappropriate. They held us accountable, they did not fear us, and they always encouraged us to do the right thing. Today's generation of adults, my generation takes very little interest in activities outside of our own homes and personal interests. In fact, this will not be a popular statement among my peers, but needs to be said nonetheless. In many African American communities it seems that during our ascent into the colleges, universities, and careers that our ancestors only dreamed about we forgot that others paved the way for us to make that ascent, and many of us fail to give back. We often forget the way our parents did more with less; we forget that our parents sacrificed so that we could have the things we needed; and we forget that our neighbors took more than a passing interest in our activities. There was a community available to us that is missing today.

The father I knew at birth left when I was ten years old. My mother raised me the best she could, but was still trying to live her life, was under equipped as a parent, and oftentimes simply had little to give. I am not judging or criticizing my mother because she gave us what she had, did the best she could with what she had, and taught me the meaning of love was more than the use of the three words 'I love you'. But because the adults in my community were involved, our neighbors took an interest in me and provided the additional support that I clearly needed. I have a friend from my youth whom I cannot even remember meeting. We learned to ride our big wheels together; we learned to play sports together; we started school together; and we were regulars in each other's homes for as far back as I can remember.

My friend's mother passed away a couple of years ago. As I sat in her funeral, I remembered when we were young she worked at the post office. In our community she made what we thought was pretty good money. My family was extremely poor so I never had money for ice cream, or visits to McDonald's, or trips to the circus, or to go to the mall and do what other kids my age were doing. Recognizing this, my friend's mother made sure that I was always able to experience the things my friends were experiencing. Whether kids were going to the mall, the movies, or ball games, I always was able to go. This was huge for me. My best friend at the time never went to any of those places without me. His mom always made sure to take me along also. Think about what that means for a moment. This woman took more than a passing interest in her son's friend. She took responsibility for her son's friend. Being an adult now with children of my own I am constantly reminded of how difficult that must have been for her. She treated me as if I were her own son, and not once was I ever made to feel like an imposition.

Another childhood friend whose mom died when we were still young, had an older sister, who did the same thing. My first trip to Marshall Field's in Chicago's famous Water Tower was with my friend's sister, where she purchased outfits for me at the same time she purchased them for him. In addition to his older sister, my friend also had an older brother who would punch me in the chest whenever he got word of me misbehaving. A neighbor, who had lost her own son in a swimming incident would call me "Sidney the good boy" and always tell me that I was special. She gave me treats and hugs all the time, but would not hesitate to reprimand me when she saw me misbehaving, reminding me constantly that I was created for greatness. These are just a few examples of an entire "village" in which I grew up where adults provided the kind of love and support for me and my peers that is clearly not being provided for the young people of today.

In today's generation, I have seen adults walk past two six year old boys fighting and do nothing to stop them. I watched a 1st grader crying as he was being beaten up by a group of boys as he walked down the street trying to go home, while adults walked past and did nothing. We are not talking about teens where breaking up a fight could get one hurt. We are talking about children under ten years old. So, my generation wants to turn a blind eye to the things we see children doing to others, and then asks what's wrong with them when their behavior affects us. When it is our child being beaten up by several boys we want something done about it, yet when we see it happening to someone else's child, "it is not our problem". The first thing that has to change in order for us to help this generation of young people is the thought process that says this is not my problem. Dr. Martin Luther King, Jr. said, "Injustice anywhere is a threat to justice everywhere". The "not my problem attitude" corrupts any relationship that could develop between adults and children, and creates the kind of inconsistency from adults that leads young people to distrust them.

When we explore closely the issues affecting today's young people, it becomes clear that primarily what is needed is a shift in attitude on the part of the adults; an awakening, in which adults, especially those who work directly with youth, but those who encounter them in general also, begin to realize that these children's personal problems are all of our problems. Until the personal problems are dealt with, any efforts at educating, socializing, training, or employing them will be severely hampered by unresolved issues, and promising young people will continue to become menaces to society rather than productive members of society. Those of us who work closely with these children have to lead the charge to convince the world of this fact.

Behaviors to avoid

In addition to the "not my problem" attitude, there has also developed in our society a competitive-based selfishness that causes individuals to worry more about their personal advancements and less about the collective. It can be seen clearly in team sports where star athletes are commonly forced to defend themselves against allegations of caring more about their individual numbers than the team's overall success. While this selfishness has been known to divide professional sports teams, it also contributes greatly to the sense of divide, distrust and disconnect that currently exists between young people and adults. I have heard several students with whom I have worked say, "my mom or my dad is so involved in their own life that they do not even pay attention to what I'm doing." Another popular comment from children is, "nobody cares anyway". Students who are heard making such statements should be prime targets for mentoring. There are several things that mentors can do once identification has been made to begin the process of repairing the disconnect that exist between children and adults. There are a few behaviors you should avoid in order to re-establish the trust of your youth:

Judgmental attitudes: Children receive criticism as judgmental when they believe adults are forcing the adult's values onto them. An example of this would be suggesting to a young lady who is considered a Tomboy that she dresses more "like a lady". Such suggestions can cause the young lady to think something is wrong with the way she currently dresses, and may reinforce feelings of low self-esteem leading the young lady to believe she needs to change some part of herself in order to be fully accepted by the adult because she is not good enough in her present state. Such behavior will lead the young lady to disconnect from the adult rather than change her attire.

Insensitivity to the issues that may be affecting them: If a mentor knows that a child has a mother who is an alcoholic and the child misbehaves constantly, then the mentor should be sensitive to the behavior the child may be experiencing at home as a result of the mother's issues. Insensitivity to these kinds of issues can make a child feel like you do not understand and because you do not understand you are unable to help them.

When a child discusses an issue with you, be present. Make the child believe that the issue you are discussing with them at that moment is the only thing that matters. Whether you believe the issue is serious or not, remember it is serious for the child and therefore it needs to be serious to you. There may be times when one of your students need to talk and you are busy with reports, grants, budgets, grading papers, or some other administrative duty and just do not have time to talk at that moment. The temptation may be to listen, while you work on your paperwork. However, the better response is to stop working on your paperwork, gauge the seriousness of the topic, and based on the seriousness of the topic, either postpone the paperwork or schedule a time later to talk to the child.

Violating their trust: We will discuss this in greater detail in subsequent chapters, but the point cannot be emphasized enough. When a child shares information with you, remember that the information being shared is for you. Definitely do not share it with any other children, and if it does not create danger for the child, then do not share it with any adults either. Remember, oftentimes children believe they do not have anyone in whom they can confide. If they open up to and confide in you and you violate their trust, it may be years before they are able to trust again, and you may have blown the opportunity for them to trust you with more serious issues in the future.

Responding with an attitude of indifference: "I am going to get paid whether you do it or not." I have heard these words uttered numerous times by frustrated adults. However, while these are some of the most common words uttered by frustrated adults, they are some of the most damaging words adults can say to children. The message the adult sends the child is "I do not care about you. I am just here to get paid." That message will cause the child to shut down and will destroy any hopes the adult has of working effectively with them again in the future.

Avoiding these kinds of mistakes will help you be the kind of adult that young people will feel like they can confide in. It will be that confidence in you that will allow you to be the kind of mentor that can help them.

The quote by Tatum O' Neal in the beginning of this chapter speaks volumes about the cycle of abuse being experienced by many young people. "If these things are being allowed to happen to me then it just seems normal to continue to do them to myself." Many "troubled" youth suffer from this mindset. We will talk extensively about untreated mental illness and unresolved social and family issues being the root cause of some of the behaviors we see. However, the quote by Tatum O' Neal reveals the truth that "troubled" youth are not limited to racial or economic conditions. One of the things I tell my students is that everybody has a story and most people are so busy living their story that they could not care less about yours. EVERYBODY HAS A STORY! The poor kid who comes to school misbehaving and snatching food from his fellow students may not be eating at home. The rich kid who is arrogant and looks his nose down on others may have a father who works so much that he spends no time with his son, leaving the son to seek attention elsewhere. The dark complexioned kid may have a complex because other kids have talked about how dark he is. The bi-racial kid may have a problem because he does not feel like he fits in with either of his cultures. The shy kid may have been teased for having bad breath and so he feels awkward talking a lot around strangers. The bottom line when communicating with your students is that under no circumstance can you allow them to use their story as an excuse. If everybody has a story, then the message for the children we mentor is "**We have to rise above our story.**"

Treat the problems, not the symptoms

As caring adults, while not allowing them to use their story as an excuse, under no circumstance can we deny the impact that their story is having on them. For example, if we see a young girl who has amazing potential, but has a very troubled home life, then we have to know that the home life is impacting the behavior. Therefore, when we see the young lady veer off course, we do not berate her, we instead re-direct her based on the sensitivity of our prior knowledge of her home life. If we see an otherwise calm young man who we know comes from a family heavily engaged in gang activity constantly getting into scuffles with other children, then we know that the child is being impacted by the message he is getting at home. So when he gets into scuffles, rather than condemn him we need to re-direct him based on our prior knowledge of his situation. So, in other words, what I am proposing is while we do not allow them to use their stories as excuses, we cannot ignore those stories either. Their stories should strengthen and empower us. These stories should build our tolerance, allowing us to work with these "troubled" youth until we can see beyond the symptoms being expressed in their behavior. Once we have seen past the surface and identified the bigger issues, we can then place them into programs, and offer services that address the issues that have been identified in those stories.

We know that a young lady who has been molested as a child may become promiscuous. We know that a child who was heavily condemned at home may become overly critical. We know that a child who did not receive nurturing and caring at home may need extra validation. We know that a child who lives in fear will not want to take chances. We know that a child who lives in an environment where there is a lot of hostility will learn to fight. So promiscuity, overly critical behavior, people pleasing, apprehension, and fighting are the behaviors that we see, but they are symptoms of the problems that exist and are separate from the problems themselves. If we fail to make this distinction, we will spend all of our time treating symptoms, yet failing to see noticeable progress with our students because the problems will always find a way to manifest through other symptoms. So, for example we may help the young girl get over her promiscuity but she may then have outbursts of anger; same problem, different symptom. Until the young girl deals with her molestation, and begins to heal the scars associated with it, the issues that derive from the molestation will always find a way to show themselves again. Fungus grows as long as it is in the dark. However, the moment it is exposed to light, it loses its power and dies. So too are the issues that affect behavior. As long as they are buried in the dark recesses of the mind, they control behavior, but the moment they are exposed to the light of awareness they lose their power and die. Our role as mentors is to expose the fungus in the minds of our young people so that the fungus can die freeing the minds of our young people to live happy, productive lives.

Chapter Two

Tackling the Mental Health Giant

"For too long we have swept the problems of mental illness under the carpet... and hoped that they would go away."

Richard J. Codey

Many of the children with whom you come into contact may suffer from a variety of mental health disorders through which you may have to navigate in order to help them. We will take a close look at some of the most common disorders, and identify ways concerned adults can work with children who suffer from these various disorders. Unfortunately, mental health is not given the attention it deserves in many communities. Particularly, this is true in African American communities, where in many circles, mental health issues are viewed as lack of faith, or weakness, or even as excuses for personal shortcomings. We will take a close look at a few particularly common disorders I have seen in many of the youth with whom I have worked and ways that caring adults can support the children who suffer from them so that they may overcome the stigmas associated with these disorders and receive the help they need in order to have a chance to become productive citizens.

The lack of mental health support currently available is especially disturbing, considering the fact that the American Academy of Child & Adolescent Psychiatry has reported that about five percent of children and adolescents in the general population suffer from depression at any point in time. Particularly, the academy reports that children under stress, and those who have attention, learning, conduct and anxiety disorders are at an even higher risk for depression. Depression, however is only one of the mental health issues facing the youth of today.

There are other mental health illnesses that are making classroom management difficult for teachers, and learning nearly impossible for some students. ADHD is the most commonly diagnosed behavioral disorder of childhood. It affects nearly 5% of school aged children, and may run in families, although it is not clear exactly what causes it. Whatever the cause may be, it seems to be set in motion early in life as the brain is still developing. While there are those who do not believe in the authenticity of ADHD, "medical imaging studies have suggested that the brains of children with ADHD are in fact different from those of other children."

In addition to Depression, and ADHD, Bi-Polar Disorder is another mental health disorder that is causing problems for adults who work with children. According to the National Institute of Mental Health, Bipolar disorder is a serious brain illness, also referred to as manic-depressive illness. Children with bipolar disorder go through unusual mood changes. Sometimes they feel very happy or "up," and are much more active than usual. This is called mania. And sometimes children with bipolar disorder feel very sad and "down," and are much less active than usual, which of course is called depression. Bi-Polar disorder causes those who suffer from it to experience extreme emotions. According to the American Foundation of Suicide Prevention, over 2 million Americans suffer from Bi-Polar disorder. Many are children and working with them can be extremely challenging without proper training.

However, probably the least diagnosed, but most damaging disorder affecting children with whom you are likely to engage as "troubled" is Post-Traumatic Stress Disorder. Post-Traumatic Stress Disorder is most commonly associated with military war veterans. However, it is an emotional illness that is classified as an anxiety disorder, and usually develops as a result of a terribly frightening, life-threatening or otherwise highly unsafe experience. Statistics regarding PTSD indicate that 7 – 8% of the population will likely develop PTSD at some point in their lifetime. However, due to the effects of poverty and educational deficiencies previously discussed these numbers are much higher in marginalized communities from which many of the "troubled" students will come.

Before we begin to identify ways to cope with mental health disorders among some of our "troubled" children, it is important to note that I am not a clinician. This guide is not intended as a substitute for a clinical evaluation done by a professional. In fact, the exact opposite is true; it is highly recommended that someone with clinical mental health training conducts a thorough investigation to positively identify the issue a child is dealing with whenever possible. However, although we are not clinicians, caring, attentive adults are often the first line of defense in identifying issues, and therefore should be trained in: how to identify specific disorders; the side effects and behavior caused by these disorders; the types of treatments that are available for each disorder; and the role of mentoring and social service agencies in treatment. Having said that, I have examined some of the disorders I have encountered and ways I have found to support the children who suffered from them.

Depression

Depression is one of the more common types of mood disorders in children, although sometimes not taken seriously due to the connotation of the word. When people feel down because something bad has happened, they are said to be depressed. However, the form of depression that affects everyone at some point in life when something bad happens is not the same as the mood disorder depression. The mood disorder is defined by NIMH as an illness in which the feelings of depression persist for extended time periods to the point where they interfere with a person's ability to function in everyday life. When children or young adults suffer from depression, their behavior is usually slightly different than adults who may suffer from the disease. Children however, who may not have the option of turning to drugs or alcohol as a means of self-medicating, are often much better at masking the symptoms of their depression. If you suspect a child you work with may suffer from depression, look for the following signs:

- Frequent sadness
- Inability to enjoy previously enjoyable activities

- Hopelessness
- Low energy
- Low self-esteem and guilt
- Extreme sensitivity to perceptions of rejection and failure
- Irritability
- Complaints of physical ailments like headaches, and stomachaches
- Poor concentration
- Drug or alcohol abuse
- Thoughts of suicide or other self-destructive behavior

Also, remember when looking at a child's behavior that a child who causes frequent problems at school, after school, or even at home may be doing so because of depression. When working with children who display negative behavior, ask them how they feel. If they respond that they feel unhappy, angry, sad, or another such emotion, they may be suffering from depression. It is extremely important to the children who you work with that you are aware and pay close attention to the warning signs. Early diagnosis and treatment are essential for helping children who suffer from depression. Remember that the child may not just feel bad, but may actually suffer from a life threatening illness that may require professional help.

A person experiencing a major depressive episode navigates through life with the equivalence of a paraplegic. Imagine a paraplegic going through life without a wheelchair, without handicap accessible facilities, and given no other accommodations for his disability. In fact, what if no one even acknowledged the disability? How difficult would life be for the paraplegic? This degree of difficulty defines the everyday life of a child experiencing a major depressive episode.

Teens are particularly susceptible to depression due to the normal physical changes the body undergoes during puberty. In addition to the normal challenges of physical development are the psychological and emotional challenges of trying to find out who they are and where they fit into the world. They are developing their own ideologies and set of values that may or may not agree with the ones that they had been taught. It is vital during these developmental years that teens acquire a strong sense of self through the support of parents and other caring adults, making the role of coaches and mentors vital in their development. However, due to the variety of changes and personal development, it sometimes makes it difficult to assess whether a teen is depressed or just going through typical teenaged moodiness. If you have a teen who you suspect may be depressed, observe the previously mentioned warning signs and consider how long the symptoms have been present, the severity of the symptoms, and just how different the teen is behaving. Remember, when observing the teen in question that some symptoms may be a part of the teen's normal development, but dramatic changes in personality, mood, and behavior that are long-lasting are red flags that something is going on with the teen. Some additional things to look for in teens who may suffer from depression as they seek ways to deal with their emotional pain are:

Problems in school – The low energy and concentration difficulties caused by depression may lead to poor attendance, a decline in overall academic performance, and a lack of interest from a teen who was once a good student.

Running away – Many depressed teens run away from home or talk about running away from home. These attempts to escape are actually a cry for help.

Ugly comments – Low self-esteem is often a trigger for depression, and can often be identified through hearing a teen who once had a healthy sense of self make comments about being ugly, unattractive, or unworthy.

Internet addiction – Isolation is a sign of depression and with teens may be expressed through an obsession with the internet. Just as drugs and alcohol are used to escape what is perceived as a painful reality, the internet is another way of escape. However, also like the drugs and alcohol, excessive use of the internet leads to further isolation and often makes them feel even more depressed.

Reckless behavior – Depressed teens may engage in high risk behaviors, such as promiscuous sexual activity, practicing unsafe sex, out of control drinking, drug use, reckless driving, and violence, including self-mutilation. In one of my programs, we had a young lady who would cut herself because she was depressed over the lack of acceptance brought on by her lesbian relationship.

Once a caring adult has suspicions that a child or teen is suffering from depression there are several things the adult can and should do to help the child.

Offer emotional support – The best thing you can do for a child whom you believe is suffering from depression is to be there for them in a non-judgmental role. Remember that children are looking for relationships in which they can be accepted as they are.

Speak to the parents – This can be difficult, especially when parents are in denial about what is going on with their child. However, oftentimes parents are either the last to notice behavioral changes in their child, or they notice but are confused about what they can do to help the child. A mental health referral from a Youth Development Professional, teacher, or other caring adult may be exactly what the parent needs to get the ball rolling.

Speak to the school – This is a way to guarantee that the child will receive some assistance. The school will have access to Licensed Clinical Social Workers and Psychiatrists who will be able to conduct thorough assessments and make professional recommendations. The school will also have access to resources to assist the child in getting whatever continued treatment the child will need.

Be willing to listen – The tendency to give advice when working with young people can be overwhelming. In fact, most of the time it is a good thing for a teen to receive advice from a caring, responsible adult.

However, when suffering from depression sometimes teens will shut down completely. So, when they are willing to talk, and re-open communication lines, it is good to just let them pour out their feelings, without comment.

Validate feelings – Avoid the desire to talk the child out of their depression. Even when you have great intentions; even when the child is completely off base; and even when you know they are being irrational, just acknowledge that their pain is real. If you do not they will feel like you do not take their feelings seriously, and you will run the risk of them shutting down again. Remember you want to keep them talking. Talk them off the ledge but do not dismiss their pain.

Although relatively common and treatable, if left untreated, depression can be very damaging, leading to difficulty in relationships, and oftentimes thoughts of suicide, homicide, and other acts of rage. Once the depression has been diagnosed and a treatment plan has been put in place, the best thing a mentor or caring adult can do is help the student follow the plan. This can be difficult, especially when prescription medicine is involved. The medication may cause other problems. For example antidepressants, while extremely helpful with patients with suicide ideation, may not be necessary in cases of mild depression, and may bring additional problems with its side effects. Research the illness as much as possible so that you can provide your parents with accurate information so that the parents can then make informed decisions about the welfare of their child. However, once medication has been prescribed, make sure you inquire about how it is affecting the child, but encourage them to follow the prescription set by their doctor. While it is true that antidepressants when taken can increase the risk of suicidal thinking, it is also true that they also may cause violent episodes when missed. Be alert and watchful to determine if the behavior is getting worse, and keep the parents and school informed of your observations.

We had a young man whose home environment was not very supportive who was taking medication for depression. Once his mentor realized that no one at home was ensuring the young man take his medicine, he brought it to our attention and we made the young man's observation a collective effort. We got to know this young man so well that we could tell by his behavior when he had not taken his medication. Subsequently we could intervene before his behavior got too far out of control and re-direct him to keep him from getting himself in trouble.

Attention Deficit Hyperactivity Disorder (ADHD)

Although much information has been made available in recent years regarding Attention Deficit Hyperactivity Disorder, commonly referred to as ADHD, it is still not clear exactly what causes the disorder. ADHD may run in families, but whether this can be stated with certainty is inconclusive. However, what is clear is that it is now among the most commonly diagnosed behavioral disorder in children, affecting about 3 – 5% of school aged children. ADHD is identified as a problem with inattentiveness, over-activity, impulsivity, or a combination of these issues. This broad definition makes ADHD sometimes difficult to identify as many of the symptoms of ADHD are part of the normal developmental stages in children. For example, teens between the ages of 13 and 15 are developing their own value systems and beginning to test limits as part of their normal cognitive development. So, teens at a normal stage of development are experiencing some of the same issues as teens who suffer from ADHD, which makes detection and diagnosis of ADHD difficult and creates cynicism among critics, with some claiming ulterior motives of the medical industry as they argue that the disease is promoted by the same industry that promotes the use of pharmaceutical drugs for its treatment.

However, for our purpose we will discuss ADHD as a mental health disorder in which the symptoms primarily fall into three categories. Children with ADHD may fall into any one of these types, or a combination of these variations.

- Inattentiveness
- Hyperactivity
- Impulsivity

Hyperactivity and impulsivity are often discussed as one disorder. Of the three types, those diagnosed with the inattentive type are diagnosed less frequently. Although they often do not do well in school, kids with inattentive-type ADHD do not get in trouble a lot for being disruptive in class, which is why it is diagnosed less frequently than other forms of ADHD that do cause children to be disruptive. Because the lack of focus in children with Inattentive type ADHD is turned inward, they often spend time in their own dream worlds instead of talking to other students. Proper diagnosis of inattentive type ADHD is critical to a child's academic and social success. Students with the inattentive type are likely to fall behind in their schoolwork because of this disorder, and would likely be too introverted to make the kinds of solid friendships that could encourage learning. If left undiagnosed and untreated, inattentive type ADHD can leave a child feeling isolated and alone, possibly creating fear, anxiety and a host of other issues that would affect the quality of their lives, leaving them to potentially be classified as "troubled". Should you suspect any of your students suffer from Inattentive ADHD, here are some things to look for:

- Often fails to give close attention to details or makes careless mistakes in schoolwork, work, or other activities
- Often has difficulty sustaining attention in tasks or play activities
- Often does not seem to listen when spoken to directly
- Often does not follow through on instructions and fails to finish schoolwork, chores, or duties in the workplace
- Often has difficulty organizing tasks and activities
- Often avoids, dislikes, or is reluctant to engage in tasks that require sustained mental effort (such as schoolwork or homework)

- Often loses things necessary for tasks or activities (e.g., toys, school assignments, pencils, books, or tools)
- Is often easily distracted
- Is often forgetful in daily activities

Children in whom you notice several of these symptoms, but do not really notice any of the symptoms of hyperactivity may suffer from ADHD Inattentive type. The responsibility of the caring adult/mentor is not to diagnose, but to observe and report what they observe. Comprehensive evaluations should be left to qualified psychologists, psychiatrists, and other medical professionals trained to assess mental health disorders.

The good news about Inattentive ADHD according to both the American Academy of Pediatrics and the American Academy of Child and Adolescent Psychiatry is that it can be treated and children who suffer from it can live relatively normal lives. Like other mental health disorders, medication may be necessary for the treatment of Inattentive ADHD. The Center for Disease Control and Prevention (CDC) says that 70 to 80 percent of ADHD patients respond positively to stimulants. However, according to the National Resource Center on ADHD individuals with predominantly inattentive type ADHD can benefit from minor accommodations. You can assist your students through simple accommodations such as:

- Extra time to complete assignments
- Additional feedback from instructors

- Assistance in improving organizational skills
- Tutoring and techniques to improve study habits.

Many schools utilize an IEP (Individualized Education Plan) to ensure that students with developmental challenges are still getting these kinds of needs met. The IEP identifies the disorder and makes concessions to accommodate the student. For example, a student with ADHD may be given extra time to complete assignments, or a student with a learning disability may be graded on a different scale than the rest of the class. While the IEP system still has challenges: i.e. teachers being poorly trained regarding the needs of students with mental health disorders; teachers being insensitive to students' needs; and poor communication between school staff regarding the student's IEP; without it being in place, children would have an extremely difficult time trying to get the support they need.

Children who have symptoms of hyperactivity and impulsivity may present a few more challenges than the children with the inattentive type. These children may:

- Fidget and squirm in their seats
- Talk nonstop
- Blurt out answers
- Dash around, touching or playing with anything and everything in sight
- Have trouble sitting still
- Be constantly in motion
- Have difficulty doing quiet tasks or activities.

The most obvious sign of hyperactivity/impulsivity is an inability to sit still. While many children are naturally quite active, kids with hyperactive symptoms of ADHD are always moving. They may try to do several things at once, bouncing around from one activity to the next. Even when forced to sit still which can be very difficult for them their foot is tapping, their leg is shaking, or their fingers are drumming.

If you are working with a child who is hyperactive, it may take a lot of energy to get him or her to listen, complete a task, or just to sit still. The constant monitoring can be frustrating and exhausting for the adult. Sometimes you may feel like the child is running the show, and often you will feel frustrated and out of control. But there are things you can do to ease your own mind, regain control of the situation, and help the child.

Keep things in perspective. Remember that the child's behavior is related to a disorder. It is not personal, so do not sweat the small stuff. If the child is tapping their foot, or drumming their fingers and it is not causing a disturbance let them. Allowing them to do something simple like tap a foot may actually be keeping them from engaging in even more disruptive behavior.

Demonstrate belief in the child. Use positive affirmations to identify everything that is positive, valuable, and unique about the child. One of my tricks would be to take a kid who was being really disruptive and make him my assistant for the day. I would give the kid authority to deliver my messages to staff and to oversee projects and everything. By the end of the day, the kid is usually so excited that they begin to act better on their own, just from having someone demonstrate belief in them.

Take care of yourself. Working with youth who suffer from ADHD can be extremely stressful. Find ways to reduce stress levels, whether it means taking a nightly bath or practicing morning meditation. Remember if you are not healthy, you cannot be of any help to the child.

Build a support base. One of the most important things to remember in working with a child with ADHD is that you cannot do it alone. Talk to others about ways of being supportive of children with ADHD. Make it a regular part of your training and staff discussions. Seek clinical assistance in developing strategic plans for helping this population.

Take breaks. Do not feel like a failure for walking away. One of the major benefits of building a support base is that you do not have to try and be everything for that child. When you feel overwhelmed, ask for help, and walk away when help arrives. You can always come back when you have calmed down.

Establish structure with clearly defined rules and consequences. Children with ADHD are more likely to succeed in completing tasks when the tasks occur in predictable patterns and in predictable places. Your job is to help create and sustain an environment that provides that structure. All children function better when the rules are clear and the consequences are understood. However, this is particularly true for children with

ADHD. It is important to explain what will happen when the rules are obeyed and when they are broken. Then, stick to your system: follow through each and every time with a reward or a consequence consistent with what you have told them.

Hyperactivity/impulsive behavior can be one of the most challenging disorders for a teacher or mentor to handle, especially when they are responsible for a number of other students as well. However, this is an issue for which a mentor should definitely be prepared to provide assistance to a child. Use the one on one time that you get with your students to address some of the suggestions for help to reinforce for the students the importance of following those suggestions. Also, keeping accurate notes on what you and the student discussed and accomplished could provide important information for therapists, parents, and teachers. As always, if you know medication has been prescribed consistently inquire (in private) about whether the child is taking it. Be thorough, consistent, and patient with the student struggling with ADHD and you will be surprised how much you are able to help that child.

Bi-Polar Disorder

Bi-polar disorder is a serious brain illness, also referred to as manic-depression. Children who suffer from bi-polar disorder go through unusual mood changes. They sometimes feel very happy, upbeat, and active, but then can just as quickly feel very sad, down, and depressed. Not to be confused with the normal ups and downs of childhood, children with bi-polar experience these ups and downs in extreme ways, often to the point of being a threat to themselves or others. The mood changes experienced by these children are polar opposites.

Manic episodes may cause children to:

- Feel very happy or act silly in a way that is unusual
- Have a very short temper
- Talk really fast about a lot of different things
- Have trouble staying focused
- Talk about sex more often
- Engage in risky behavior

Children having depressive episodes may:

- Feel sad for no obvious reason
- Complain of headaches or stomachaches
- Feel guilt or worthlessness for no explainable reason
- Overeat or eat very little
- Have little energy
- Talk about death or suicide

One of the things I have noticed in working with children with bi-polar disorder is that there is not a grace period to identify when the bi-polar disorder will kick in. Mood changes can occur suddenly, and without warning. We had a student who suffered from bi-polar disorder who was a junior in high school when we met her. She was really a sweetheart. At the particular school I was working at the time, the students who were classified as Special Education were bused to school. I remember standing talking to her one day, having a pleasant conversation with her, when the bus driver came in to find out why this student was not yet on the bus. In fairness to the young lady, the driver came through the door and called her name, very loudly and very aggressively. He then said, also very loudly and very aggressively, "HURRY UP, I AIN'T GOT ALL DAY TO WAIT ON YOU." The young lady snapped. Just as calmly as she had been standing there talking to me, she was equally explosive in her response to him. "Don't you see me talking to my mentor, you don't f*% ing talk to me like that." She went on and on in a profanity laden tirade that lasted several minutes, in the middle of the hallway, where other students were present. I had a great relationship with this student, but try as I may, I could not calm her down.

This young lady would go on to have similar explosions against members of our staff, and these explosions would be without incident. So, no one would provoke her, as in the case of the driver. She would just have moments where she would explode. It became overwhelming for the young lady who was her assigned mentor. The child would on the one hand want to be with her mentor so much that she would skip classes to find her. Then, she would curse the mentor out in almost the very next moment. The mentor, as much as she wanted to help this student would eventually ask me to replace her with another mentor, as she felt like she was no longer able to help this girl. Eventually, this young lady was transferred into a therapeutic school where she was able to get the on-going support she needed. What we found out about this young lady was that she was not taking her medication consistently, and as a result, she was having frequent episodes. What we found out about working with children with bi-polar disorder was that even when the desire to help them was present, knowledge of the disorder, and wisdom to apply the knowledge were essential for the mentor to sustain any efforts at helping that child. We replaced the previous mentor with one with a more clinical background who understood the disorder, and she was able to help the child better fit in for the duration of the time she was with us. In fact, the student asked her parent, and was allowed to continue working with us even after she had transferred to the therapeutic school.

One of the most important things to remember about students who suffer from bi-polar disorder is that their mood episodes are intense. They may last a week or two, or sometimes even longer. In the case of our example, we knew about the disorder, which helped us deal with the mood swings. However, knowing about the disorder did not lessen the impact of it, which is why it takes extreme discipline and focus on the part of the adult to ignore the outbursts. The most important thing for the adult is to remember that the child has a disorder. Reminding themselves of this should build their tolerance levels which should help the mentor abstain from any emotional response that may come from the child's outbursts. Some basic things an adult can do when working with a child who suffers from bi-polar disorder are:

- Be patient
- Encourage the child to talk, and listen intently when they do
- Understand the mood episodes
- Inquire about medication
- Ignore the outbursts
- Help the child have fun

Although there are no cures for bi-polar disorder, on-going treatment can help control symptoms. The types of on-going treatment needed will probably be based on a multitude of factors, including the complexity of the symptoms. Medication of some form will almost always be required. Make sure that as the mentor you understand the medication that has been prescribed, the dosage amount, and the possible side effects. Share this information with other members of your team as well as the school. Any side effects that you notice should be reported to the parents and school immediately. Also, suggest to parents that psychotherapy can be effective in helping children with bi-polar disorder. Therapy helps children establish and manage a routine that works for them. Once therapy has begun, an effective mentor will reinforce any progress established during the psychotherapy. A private chart is a great tool to share with other staff members, parents, and teachers that tracks the moods and behaviors of the child. This tool, when shared with parents will be an effective way to help parents: track the effectiveness of medical doses; communicate with doctors so that treatment plans can be altered as needed; and create a support system of caring adults for the student and ensure that the entire team is on the same page.

Post-Traumatic Stress Disorder (PTSD)

PTSD is an emotional disorder that is classified as an anxiety disorder. This disorder is generally associated with military veterans, however the symptoms cannot be ignored when analyzing them against children who grow up in poverty ridden communities and abusive and neglectful homes. Consider that victims of PTSD:

- Have lived through frightening, life threatening, emotional, highly unsafe experiences.
- Re-experience the traumatic event or events in some way over and over again.
- Avoid places, people, or other things that remind them of the event.
- Are extremely sensitive to normal life experiences.
- Live lives characterized by long lasting problems with social and emotional functioning.

Typically, when discussing or considering this disorder people tend to think of traumatic events like witnessing someone get killed, getting raped as a child, losing a loved one, a near death experience, or some other form of *severe* trauma. However, often overlooked are the not so dramatic experiences that are no less traumatic for the individuals who survive them. PTSD can be a major stumbling block for progress in working with a child from a troubled home or one living in extreme poverty, and can often go undiagnosed. I know firsthand, the devastation this disorder can cause.

I was born and raised on the south side of Chicago in a less than ideal situation. I was raised in a single family home from the time I was around 8 or 9 years old. My mother, who worked much of my early life, did the best she could but she was not a very nurturing mother, and quite frankly lacked some of the parenting skills needed to develop healthy, confident children. It was not that my mother did not care, or that she did not want to be nurturing, it was because like many of the parents we see, she had issues of her own that had never been addressed and resolved. She did not grow up in the home with her own mother; she was molested growing up, and nothing was ever done; she lived in the house with a grandfather who could be mentally and verbally abusive; and she was emotionally abused, and mistreated by 3 different husbands. So my mother did the best she could with what she had to work with but her own reality limited her ability to provide for me the things I needed from her. However, while I understand all of that now from an intellectual point of view, the truth of the matter is that my intellectual understanding does not negate the emotional damage that was done. In spite of my mother's intentions, like many of the parents of "troubled" youth, she lacked the ability to create the kind of environment that children need to grow up healthy, strong, and confident. As a result of dysfunction in the home, like other "troubled" youth, I too would develop issues.

We were extremely poor growing up so I never had the latest fashions; and I often appeared dirty and disheveled. I had an extremely big head. In fact I often joke that my head is the same size today as it was when

I was ten years old. This combination of issues made me a regular target of teasing by my peers. This constant teasing, which happened daily, made me very self-conscious of my appearance and filled me with feelings of self-doubt, inadequacy, and even inferiority. The problem with peer teasing is if the person being teased is not being reinforced at home, or from some other caring adult, then they begin to internalize the comments being made about them. This is what happened to me. Although I had adults in the community who encouraged me, I was not being encouraged at home, and eventually this would take its toll. In addition to the day to day teasing I endured were two major events that happened that would shape the next few decades of my life.

The first event happened when I was about five years old. I was sitting on the porch with a neighbor who was maybe 11 or 12 years old at the time. I remember her being a very sweet girl. However, on this particular day she had several of her friends who stopped by while we were sitting there. I am not quite sure how it started, but these kids started to talk about me. At first, they made a few comments that were met with a few chuckles. I even laughed myself at a couple of the comments. But somewhere along the way, the joking turned bad and I no longer found it funny. My sensitivity to the joking was ignored and seemed to even fuel the kids to continue talking about me, and to do so even more harshly. I am not sure how long this went on, but I do know that it continued until I was in tears. However, my tears did not slow them down, but fueled them on even more. The young lady who was their friend even tried to stop them. Like lions fighting a struggling gazelle, who had tasted blood, they proceeded. This went on for a while, and ended with me bawling uncontrollably. I struggled through the tears to find my way into the house, where my mother struggled to find out what was wrong with me. She was able to calm me down long enough to explain to her what happened. Her response was, "is that what you are crying about? Boy please, you are going to have a lot more to cry about than somebody talking about you. Go sit down and watch TV." She did not go out and look for the kids who did this to me. She did not take me in her arms and comfort me. She did not even say that those kids were out of order and tell me to ignore them. She said, that what I experienced was nothing compared to what I had in store for me. This was my introduction to an inferiority complex. What my mother taught me in that moment was that it was okay for people to treat me that way, and at five, I reasoned that the reason it was okay was because I deserved it.

The second incident occurred in 1981. I was 11 or 12 years old and we were going to my sister's high school graduation. My sister went to Morgan Park high school in Chicago, which was probably 50/50 at the time in terms of racial demographics between black and white students. My sister was extremely beautiful, smart, and had done well in school, winning several awards her senior year. She had even qualified for college and would be leaving to go to Western Illinois University in the fall. My grandmother had 14 children, and numerous grandchildren and to my knowledge my sister was the first to go to college. Needless to say, this was an extremely proud time for our family. However, it would not end well for me. While we were at the graduation, a young man, probably around 16 or 17 years old, who happened to be Caucasian noticed me from across the room. He pointed at me and then got the attention of a friend of his and pointed me out to the friend. They whispered something and then began to crack up from laughter. I do not know what they discussed, but I do know that they continued to point at me and laugh. I looked around for my mom, sister, or some other friendly face, but I found none. I found a corner and stood in it, but I could not escape their eyes, and therefore was subjected to their laughter as well. This was the first of many times where I would feel like I wanted to be invisible. While I could not figure out exactly what they were laughing at, I could conclude based on their pointing gestures that it had something to do with the way I looked. Again, I reasoned that if they could not see me, then they could not laugh at me. This incident reinforced an inferiority complex that began at five, was nurtured throughout the years, was driven home at 12, and followed me the better part of my life, in the process costing me jobs, destroying relationships, and making me a classic underachiever and excuse maker, and contributing to the creation of a "troubled" youth..

After the second incident, at 12 years old, I tried to learn how to exist without being noticed. I found what I later discovered Ralph Ellison called the benefits of invisibility. I discovered that I can hide from the pain as long as I remembered the truth in the words of Ellison, "I remember that I'm invisible and I walk softly" In walking softly, I told myself, I would avoid the controversy that would bring about the teasing, and thereby avoid the pain that would result from the teasing.

The combination of these two incidents, and the years of emotional teasing and psychological torture I endured, resulted in creating in me a sense of self-loathing that existed years after the incidents had passed.

I share my personal story, for the same reason I share the stories of the young people, to demonstrate the process of how one becomes "troubled", as well as the difficult road of redemption to becoming whole again. When considering the damage that can be caused by a traumatic event going unaddressed, consider that I am 43 years old at the time of this writing. I am educated, have initiated programs, directed organizations, trained thousands of people in concepts of youth development, supervised countless staff members, raised thousands of dollars for various causes, both here and abroad, supported a family, won awards, appeared on television shows, sat on panels, been consulted by many for my expertise, met numerous professional athletes, and mentored dozens of people over the years, and yet I still battle self-esteem issues. These issues often create feelings of anxiety and inadequacy that I still have to guard against to this day.

The two incidents I described affected me so deeply that even after years of self-help, including finding a spiritual practice that works for me, and several wonderful people whom God has placed on my life path, I still struggle with feelings of insecurity and inadequacy. For years if I walked into a room and people started laughing, I would instantly think they were laughing at me. I would sweat heavily when surrounded by strangers. I would have bad dreams from which I would wake up drenched in sweat. In other words, I would relive these events over and over again, and I would suffer almost as greatly when reliving these events as I did when they occurred. So, even though I knew the traumatic events that were causing my pain, I still had not addressed them, and they therefore maintained their control over me, creating by definition Post Traumatic Stress Disorder.

I believe that my childhood traumas created in me a sense of low self-esteem and self-worth, which can be identified as the after effects of PTSD, and which were at the core of years of struggles and bad decisions. I believe my story would probably be pretty indicative of the kinds of stories one would find when examining some of today's "troubled" youth. Many of today's youth are suffering from similar traumatic stories which when viewed in perspective can be categorized as Post Traumatic Stress Disorder. Part of the challenge in working with these students is that the majority of the children you will encounter who suffer from PTSD will probably be as undiagnosed as I was.

Children who suffer from PTSD have a difficult time socially and emotionally. PTSD occurs when trauma is life threatening or severely compromises the physical or emotional well-being of an individual causing them to live in intense fear. While experts offer examples such as witnessing an accident, receiving a life threatening diagnosis, being the victim of kidnapping, exposure to combat or some natural disaster, or getting mugged or raped, events such as being left alone or neglected, being born to drug addicted parents, and being teased, and living in poverty can be equally damaging. In fact, if you are wondering how many of your children are suffering from PTSD, consider the risk factors:

- Number of traumatic events endured
- Duration of traumatic events
- Severity of the trauma experienced
- Emotional issues prevalent prior to the traumatic event
- Limited social and emotional support available from friends and family

If your children are living in or from areas of high poverty, chances are good that a lot of these factors may apply to them. When viewed in this perspective, and considering the degree of disconnect they probably feel as a result, it is no wonder that so many of our youth join gangs, use drugs, or engage in other self-destructive practices. If left untreated, which in most cases as we have already discussed, it probably is left untreated and undiagnosed, sufferers of PTSD are in store for long and difficult lives. Some of the challenges they may face include:

- Drug addiction
- Difficulty sleeping
- Poor concentration
- Persistent feelings of guilt, shame and hopelessness
- Irritability
- Suicidal thoughts
- Anxiety
- Avoidance issues

- Nightmares
- Blackouts

PTSD is the kind of disorder in which caring adults should really become familiar. One of the major reasons it goes undiagnosed is that it is difficult to assess since those who suffer from it are generally concerned with what they believe are symptoms of some other problem rather than anxiety deriving from a traumatic experience. Symptoms being treated often include body aches, depression, and/or addiction. Mentors and caring adults are perfect sources for pointing parents in the direction of PTSD as we are the ones most likely to make a child comfortable enough to share these feelings and the events that caused them.

With any mental health disorder, if you suspect a child may be suffering share your concerns with both the parents and the school. Use your resources to get the child whatever help he or she may need. However, if you want to be received well by the parents, be respectful of the sensitive nature of the topic. Doing so will allow you to help the parents overcome the stigmas of mental health disorders and together you will be able to help in the development of the kind of support system the child will need.

Chapter Three

Developing Positive Relationships

"Today we are faced with the preeminent fact that, if civilization is to survive, we must cultivate the science of human relationships... the ability of all peoples, of all kinds, to live together, in the same world, at peace."
Franklin D. Roosevelt

Developing Positive Relationships with the Students

In order to be effective in efforts to work with young people, especially in inner-cities and areas of high poverty, it is imperative that positive relationships are developed with several different key individuals in the child's life, including and most importantly the child himself. A relationship is a specific *connection* between objects, concepts, or entities. Typical forms of relationships are social relationships between people, causal relationships between events, i.e. lightening striking a tree, and mathematical or theoretical relationships between components, i.e. a motor and a car.

In youth development, the relationship that develops between a child and their mentor is the foundation of the mentor/mentee dynamic, and provides the greatest opportunity for helping the child. It will be extremely difficult for any adult, in spite of their intent to help a child when a connection is not there and no relationship has been established. Developing that connection is the single greatest factor in getting the child to buy into a mentoring relationship. The buy-in from the child is essential to any chance at progress. It is also the greatest chance for an adult to engage a child in the kind of high impact conversations that can lead to even greater impact. Impact is the ability to have a strong effect on someone to the point of changing thinking and behavior.

When I was in high school, I was a classic underachiever. By the time I was in the 12th grade I had failed four classes. At the time, four was the maximum number of classes a student was allowed to take in summer school. So, I started my senior year needing to pass every class in order to graduate from summer school. If I were to fail any class, I would have to repeat my senior year. I ended up getting Mrs. Edna Thompson for English my senior year. Mrs. Thompson had a reputation of being one the most difficult teachers in the school. In spite of the seriousness of my academic standing, I still goofed off, gave minimal effort, and by the time we approached the end of the semester I had a 38 average in Mrs. Thompson's class. I needed a 75 to pass. I went to Mrs. Thompson and practically begged for a passing grade. I told her that I had reached the maximum number of summer school classes allowed, and an 'F' in her class meant I would have to repeat my senior year. In spite of my many absences (cuts) in her class; in spite of the fact that she had caught me cheating on my midterm test; and in spite of the fact that I had countless missing assignments, because we had a relationship Mrs. Thompson gave me a chance.

Mrs. Thompson told me that if I submitted a research paper that was acceptable she would give me a passing grade for the class. Needless to say, I was ecstatic. I had goofed off for a whole semester and all I had to do was one little paper and I had a chance to pass. So, I did the paper and turned it in. Mrs. Thompson graded it and gave it back to me with a big, red "F" on the front, with red marks throughout for grammatical errors, and misspelled words. She told me to do it over. Mrs. Thompson and I went through that process six times. Each time I re-submitted the paper, she tore it apart. Finally, after all of my numerous attempts, she passed me with a "C" on the paper, and a "D" in the class. However, the lesson she taught me was far more valuable than the passing grade I received. Mrs. Thompson called me to her desk at the end of class and asked me if I knew why she made me do the paper over so many times. I told her that I thought the paper just wasn't good enough. She said that the paper itself was not the issue. She said words that I will never forget, and started a change in my life that continues to this very day. Mrs. Thompson told me, "you are a black man in America and nobody is going to give you anything. You are going to work for everything you get in this world, or you are not going to get it."

Mrs. Thompson's words had an "impact" on me that lasted even until this day. I went to summer school that summer and received three "A's" and a "B" in the four classes I had failed. That "high impact conversation" with Mrs. Thompson had a strong effect on me to a point that it caused me to have a change in thinking, which ultimately changed my behavior. Although I still went on to make many more mistakes in my life after that, a seed was planted that produced immediate results in the improved grades, but, that also produced long term results, the evidence of which is my own life and the subsequent "impact" that I have been able to have on others. However, Mrs. Thompson had established a relationship with me prior to us having that conversation. Had the relationship not been established, not only would I have failed English, but Mrs. Thompson's ability to reach me on a deeper level would not have been possible. In fact her desire to help me may not have even been there.

So, as I began to think about what makes relationships impactful, I looked back over the years at the relationships that have given me the most impact in my life, and polled others about their relationships, and found that there are glaring similarities between what makes relationships impactful. My relationship with Mrs. Thompson was valuable for me because it taught me self-reliance. My relationship with my sister is valuable for me because she has always been there for me over the years. As I battled issues of self-esteem and struggled with acceptance she was the one person I knew I could count on for a kind word. She never judged me for needing her help, but was always quick to provide help when I needed it. My relationship with my wife is great because she knows me better than anyone, and yet she accepts me, even when I am at my worst, and loves me even when I feel unlovable. My relationships with my children are incredible, because they build me up to the point I feel like there is nothing I cannot accomplish. In fact, my oldest son listed me on his Facebook page of people to be admired alongside Dr. Martin Luther King, Jr. and Malcolm X, encouraging me to follow my dreams. One of my dear friends and lodge brothers Nathan Bryant taught me that I had the ability to move people with my words, and then empowered me with a sense of responsibility to overcome my shyness and do so. Captola Watts, a neighbor, and family friend who was more like a grandmother than a neighbor, made me feel loved, and special. We read the bible together and discussed it like adults. During those discussions, she would tell me that I was blessed with insight better than most of the adults at church. She made me believe that God had given me some gifts that He did not give to everybody, and in those gifts lived my purpose. Finally, my mother, who for the better part of my childhood was a single mom with three children, taught me resilience. I saw her battle her own demons of self-esteem and abuse, having been given up by her own mother at an early age. She suffered through abusive relationships, sub-standard housing, low paying jobs, and physical, mental and emotional turmoil, yet through it all she persevered. These relationships not only provided me with the foundation I needed to heal from my issues, but they helped shape me into the man I am today. From these relationships I have learned:

- Self-reliance
- Loyalty
- Acceptance
- Encouragement
- Direction
- Unconditional love

From looking at the relationships in my own life there are were a few lessons that I learned about developing relationships with children.

Lesson One: Children have expectations.

The first lesson in developing relationships with children is recognizing that they will have expectations of you. All of the positive relationships in my life provided valuable, necessary life lessons, and made me want to be a better person. I developed expectations of the people in my life based on the attributes they provided. However, beyond my own personal relationships, I believe that if one were to talk to a hundred people about the positive relationships in their lives, the same factors would be true. While the qualities or attributes that we get from our relationships with others may be different, the fact that we come to expect something out of our relationships is universal.

If having expectations of the people with whom we share our lives is universal, then the same assumption can be made about the children whom you mentor. Children from marginalized communities, those from single family homes, those just seeking to find themselves, and even those from so-called successful homes, all want to be loved. If we keep this in mind, we can easily create the kind of environment that will allow us the opportunity to establish wonderful, healthy, nurturing relationships with our students. And it is those relationships that can lead to the kind of high impact conversations that will allow an adult to really make a difference in the life of a child.

A common mistake adults make in trying to build relationships with children is attempting to be their friend. Children want the adults in their lives to be friendly, but not their friends. Children expect the same kind of attributes from their relationships that adults are looking for in their own. The self-reliance I learned from Mrs. Thompson, the loyalty I learned from my sister, the unconditional love I get from my wife, the direction I got from my neighbor, the encouragement I get from my best friend and children, and the resilience I learned from my mother are all attributes that children expect from the adults in their lives.

In community development there is a term called "affiliation moments" which refers to union with others, typically rooted in likeness or individual closeness instead of on assumed material advantages. If we are to reach the "troubled" youth with whom we come into contact we must understand and embrace these opportunities when they present themselves. Just as Mrs. Thompson used my circumstance and our relationship to create a teachable moment for me, it is our responsibility to seek and find teachable moments for the children in whom we come in contact. When we find opportunities to create teachable moments for our children we have to be willing to provide the same attributes we expect in our own relationships. Remember, the children are expecting it of you.

Lesson Two: Get to know the children

The second lesson, and probably the most important one in developing relationships with the children is that you have to get to know them on a personal level in a non-judgmental way. In order to get to the point in your relationship with the children that they trust you enough to engage in those life changing conversations, you must first develop relationships with them. There are several areas of focus that can help you in the development of these relationships. Getting to know the students would obviously be the first step in developing such relationships. This sounds simple, but beyond surface information can actually be quite difficult to do in many cases, especially when children have experienced abuse and are guarded.

There are simple things you can do to get to know children, in spite of their reluctance. A warm greeting for example can be a very powerful weapon. Many of the children we work with never get warm greetings. Their parents may be negligent, or unloving, or maybe even non-existent in their lives. Many of the children who come into our programs live with distant relatives, in foster homes, or with drug addicted parents or siblings. Many are homeless, and some have parents who work long hours and just do not have the time. We need to recognize that many of our children may not be getting any form of love at home, warm greetings included. We found that when we gave students hugs, were excited to see them *every* time we saw them, and were consistent and sincere in our efforts to love them, even the hardest of our students came around and started to soften. Unfortunately, the reality is that in spite of their openness and acceptance we were not able to help them all. But, the good news is that we were able to help many of them, and even with the toughest students our non-judgmental approach allowed us to plant seeds so that hopefully the next mentor they meet will not have nearly as many walls to break through as we did and will be able to continue to give that child the love they seek.

One of our students, a 17 year old girl is a prime example. This young lady dressed like boy, was always in detention, was a notorious fighter, and a completely closed book, who opened up to no one. This young lady disrupted classrooms, life skills workshops, and was often disrespectful to staff for no reason at all. Through it all, we held onto hope that we could reach her. One day while she was in detention, refusing to do her homework, her mentor and I sat and talked to her in a small area where just the three of us could hear. After months of verbal abuse and assaults, this young lady finally decided to open to us.

She shared with us her story of abuse. She dressed like a boy because she was terrified of boys from being raped on separate occasions, repeatedly by a family member and once by a stranger. A beautiful girl, she figured if she dressed like a boy, fought, talked, and acted like a boy then boys would no longer find her attractive. She reasoned if they did not find her attractive then they would not attack her.

On top of her abuse was the fact that it occurred in the home of the one family member with whom the girl could most identify, causing her to be banned from the home of that family member. The rest of the family, upset because the abuse was not handled internally, but involved the authorities, ostracized the girl and her mother. This young lady, clearly traumatized by these events took on another personality to defend herself from the hostile world that allowed these things to happen to her. Once she joined our program, and developed trust in us she was able to make improvements, but the damage was too severe to maintain any long-term success.

The young lady started going to class. She made up classes she was missing by taking internet courses. She caught up with her class and put herself on course to graduate. Even when she messed up we could see progress. She came into the facility one day after school and proceeded to agitate another young lady with whom she had some history, provoking an argument with the young lady that culminated in a physical altercation. After we broke the fight up, I sent her home. We did not see her again for maybe three weeks. Concerned about her not coming by for so long, I went by her house to check on her. When she answered the door, her first words were, "I am sorry. I thought you were mad at me."

I explained to her that I was mad at her but that did not mean that I loved her any less. I could see the smile on her face when she heard those words. This was the same young lady that just months before we did not even know could smile. She came back around of course, and we were all very excited about her as we noticed continued improvements with only occasional setbacks. We were all thrown for a loop when we heard that she had been arrested.

Apparently, she had gotten with a couple of her peers, decided they were bored and proceeded to take a taxi, and rob the driver of a whopping $38. Although they did not have a gun, the driver was sprayed with mace so it was considered an armed robbery and my girl received a three year sentence for her role. We did what we could to help her. We wrote letters, took transcripts from the school, met with her public defender, and appeared at court dates to show our support. On the day of the sentencing, the judge gave her a chance to speak, and she said, "I want to apologize to my mentors, I am sorry I let you guys down." The judge was moved by her words and told her he believed she had learned her lesson, but she still had to pay for the crime she committed. She even acknowledged responsibility when she agreed.

She has served her time and is currently enrolled in Junior College and pursuing a career as a professional boxer. This young lady remains a prime target for an adult mentor, and because of the progress she has made, her next mentor will not have nearly as many walls to break through, and will be able to see a little more progress in her development. Even though we did not get the results we wanted with her, our relationship with her still allowed us to make progress with her, and many of the others who did not have such severe issues were able to turn things around completely. Getting to know them on a real and personal level in a non-judgmental way provided us with these opportunities.

Lesson Three: Make the relationship a priority

When getting to know the children remember that the relationship you have with them will be your greatest asset in your efforts to help them. Treat it as such. Give the relationship the energy it deserves. Make time to spend with the children you mentor. People generally do not get married after the first date. Remember that relationships take time to develop. Put the time in. Take them out to lunch, or to the park, to the zoo, to the movies, to the beach, and to ball games. Share the kind of moments that people who are in relationships share together.

Know all of the kids by name: I remember the theme song for Cheers as if I just heard it, "sometimes you 'wanna' go where everybody knows your name". This song is definitely an excellent way to define relationships with the children you mentor. Knowing them by name says to them that they are important to you. Knowing them by name personalizes the relationship and separates them from all of your other children. When I met students in my program for the first time I would always ask them their name. When they told me their first name I would respond by giving their last name. They would always wonder how I knew their whole names. Once I moved into an administrative role, my opportunities to interact with the children directly was often limited. However, in spite of the number of administrative duties I always made time to study the rosters so I could learn the students' names. It always amazed the students, served as a nice ice breaker, and made the statement that having a relationship with them was important to me.

Be excited to see them: The song goes on to say, "…and they're always glad you came." People want you to be happy to see them. This is easy with some of the children. But there will definitely be some children who you will not want to see coming. They will get under your skin, and raise so much hell that you will find yourself thinking about them even when you are at home. These are the children you will not want to see coming and the ones your staff will encourage you to kick out of the program. Before you kick them out, and many of them probably deserve to be kicked out, remember these children are the ones who are most in need of your excitement. Understand that if you feel this way about not wanting to see them, and you are an advocate for youth, probably everyone else does too, and the child probably knows it. So, even if you feel that way too, find something good about them, and allow that to help you get excited when you see them. You will find that many of your "troubled" youth are creative, artistic, athletic, or natural leaders, Find their gifts and use that information to place them in programs and activities where they can be successful. Their development will help get you excited about seeing them. Doing so will help you bring down some of their walls and will open up the opportunity for you to help them.

Tell them about yourself: "You 'wanna' go where you can see troubles are all the same" People are looking for others with whom they can identify. This is one of those things that some youth workers might disagree with. Because setting boundaries is one of the points that is often emphasized in youth development trainings, some youth workers mistake telling children about themselves as a violation of boundary setting. However, some of my best relationships have come from allowing the children to get to know me better. All of my students know that I am a huge sports fan. I love the Chicago Bears football team, and all of my students know it. The Bears lost terribly one game, completely blown out. The next day when I showed up to work, the kids had hung a huge banner on my door that said Mr. Johnson is a Bears fan. We laughed about that, and to this day it is one of my fondest memories of that site. But the point is because they knew about me, they knew I was going to be upset about the loss. The relationships I shared with them were enhanced by the students' familiarity with my passions and consequently I was able to develop great relationships at that site.

Engage them: Students are engaged when they are allowed to speak freely without fear of judgment. Engagement allows adults to *really* get to know children beyond the masks that they wear. It is vital in building trust in the relationship, and will make the youth more comfortable and more likely to seek the adult when more serious discussions are needed. It says to the young person that they are not just another kid to you but you actually care about what is important to them. I had one student who I knew loved the Chicago White Sox. He would talk to me all of the time about the White Sox and why this would be the year they win the World Series. Because of our shared love of Chicago sports teams, I was able to develop quite a relationship with this young man. This was a great kid who always tried to do the right thing, but suffered from low self-esteem as he was unpopular among his peers. When the opportunity came for me to reward the students who had done well, I rewarded this student by selecting him to go on the field for a White Sox game where he was able to meet the players and even had his picture shown on the big screen during the game. He will never forget that experience, as it did wonders for his self-esteem. He currently ranks number 2 in his class and still confides in me to this day.

Talk about things they like. Remember that relationships require two way forms of communication. So the relationship should not consist of you talking and the kid listening. This will cause a kid to tune you out and begin avoiding you. Regardless to how boring, trivial, or disinterested you are in subjects the students like, you have to allow them to talk about them nonetheless. You will gain much needed insight about the students from these conversations. You will also create the kind of comfortable environment the child needs to become comfortable enough to engage in more meaningful conversations. You want the children to be as comfortable as possible talking with you. Just remember, they may not have anyone else with whom they can talk freely. If you become that person for them, your ability to help them deal with life will have increased exponentially.

Have fun. This is one of my favorite aspects of working with youth. I get to stay young. I get to act silly. I get to have fun. Whenever I get stressed from the political side of the work, I always go back and spend time with the kids. Not only does it remind me why I am in this field, but I have fun in the process. Studies show that while the average adult only laughs 15 times a day, the average child laughs close to 400 times a day. Laughter is good for a variety of reasons, but mainly it provides a temporary relief from the daily stresses in life. I cannot dance. I have two left feet, with shoes that do not fit. But, I have a Michael Jackson dance that I do that is hilarious. Whenever I get an angry youth who may be having a bad day I do that dance and it always makes them laugh and lightens the mood. Have fun, and keep them laughing.

Be yourself. This is the best advice that anyone can give to someone interested in working with youth. Your true value in being an effective youth worker is in being yourself. This keeps you from trying to do too much, but also allows the kids to see you in a real way. The kids have a saying, "real recognizes real." If you are inauthentic in your efforts to reach them, they will sense it and your efforts will be severely hampered. On the contrary, once the students recognize you as authentic, even the ones with whom you do not have great relationships will at a minimum begin to see you as a resource they can use to help themselves.

Following these steps will dramatically help you in the development of your relationships with the young people you serve, and those relationships will offer you the best opportunity to have an impact in the lives of those young people.

Developing Positive Relationships with the Parents/Guardians

In order to maximize efforts to help the children, it is also imperative that relationships are developed with the parents and guardians of the children. Efforts to help the children will be disrupted by parents/guardians when they are not included in the process. Also, the parents will impede any potential progress until they develop a sense of trust and connection with the mentor themselves. Parents of those children whom society has dubbed as troubled, often feel like because of past mistakes they have made that they are directly responsible for their children's troubles. Many of these parents, due to their own troubled pasts will be particularly difficult initially, as it will take significantly longer for trust to develop. However, in order to develop the kind of trusting relationship with the child that will be needed to effectively help the child, the mentor must be willing to take the same non-judgmental attitude into the relationship with the parents. There are three major lessons that can help you in your efforts to have relationships with the parents of your students.

Lesson One: Parents want the best for their children

The first lesson in developing relationships with the parents is to understand that most parents want what is best for their child even if they do not know what it is or how to provide it.

It is easy sometimes when you hear the stories of these children to immediately blame the parents for allowing such things to happen. However, when examined more closely, one often finds similar issues in the pasts of the parents as those issues that currently haunt the children. So, oftentimes it is not that the parents willingly allowed bad things to happen to their children, but they may have simply not known how to prevent the bad things from happening, or in many cases they may still be battling their own demons and thus do not recognize that the same demons are now haunting their children. I have gone to the homes of many parents to find them drinking alcohol in the early morning. Because of their own struggles, they may want to help their children, but just do not know how.

In some cases, parents may even equate their children's struggles with ideas of normalcy. I have heard many parents whose children were being bullied say, "he has to learn how to defend himself, or people will pick on him for the rest of his life." It never occurred to them that it was their responsibility to protect the child from those who would harm him. So, rather than approaching the teacher, or contacting the school office to file a report, or requesting a conference with the principal, parents would essentially lay the responsibility of protecting himself on to the child. This approach may have worked years ago when bullies were usually the biggest kid in class, easily identifiable, and operating independently in their role as a bully; the prevailing thought being that if you beat up the bully, he will leave you alone. However, this approach simply does not work today. Bullies today usually travel in groups; have affiliations with gangs that empower them to operate as bullies; and rather than leaving you alone, they often come back shooting. So, children today who are being bullied find a simpler solution being to join the group that is bullying them. In that group, they find protection, a sense of belonging, and confidence. They are no longer targets, and they begin to get the respect for which they had longed. When the parents no longer hear about the child being bullied they think the situation has been resolved, only to later find that they have created much worse situations for their children. In order to truly help the children in your program, relationships with the parents are absolutely necessary in order to get them to learn parenting and life skills for handling these kinds of scenarios so that the parents can help their children appropriately navigate through these kinds of situations. A friend of mine once said, "advocacy of a child is a skill one has to be taught, it is not inherent." Even high functioning parents who have good parenting skills will appreciate having a mature adult who cares about their child, available in a supportive role when the child may need them.

Lesson Two: Parents have expectations

The second lesson in developing relationships with the parents is understanding that they too have expectations of you. Just as the children who come to these programs are looking for some of the various qualities we have discussed in their relationships with the staff, so too are the parents coming with their own set of expectations. One of the primary expectations that most parents will have is that you will share any information with them concerning their child. Parents want to be informed. They do not like to be surprised. I remember working in a school and going through training on handling emergencies with students when first aid has to be administered. One of the first things we learned was the importance of contacting the parent after the incident. The policy of the school I worked at the time was to treat the injury first, and call the parent second. A lot of time was spent on this policy. I understand now that the reason so much time was spent on this seemingly simple policy was to drive home the point that parents want to know. I saw a parent come to the school and find that their child had fallen and scraped a knee at recess, and they were absolutely livid because they had not been notified. Likewise, I remember a parent coming to the school whose son had ran into a brick wall during recess. Her son had a knot on his head, as big as a golf ball. However, because she had been notified, and therefore was able to mentally prepare herself, she was extremely calm when she arrived at the school.

Many of the students in the program will share information with you that they do not share with anyone else. Understanding when to be forthright with information to the parents, and when to maintain the confidentiality of the child will be necessary for any mentor to be effective. A rule of thumb I go by is to never promise a child that I will keep a secret, and never promise a parent that I will tell them everything. I make it clear with the child that my willingness to keep the secret is going to be based on whether I believe doing so will keep them safe. Likewise, I also tell the parents that any information I hear concerning their child, that I believe will put the child in danger, will be shared with them immediately. This allows me to respect the friendship and confidentiality of the child, while recognizing a concern of the parent. This is vital because once a child believes you have violated his confidence, it will be next to impossible to get it back, and once a parent feels like you are enabling their child by harboring secrets, they will prevent you from working with that child. This is a fine line that has to be treaded carefully.

We had a young lady who was extremely troubled. Her mother had been addicted to drugs during the child's early years, and as a result custody was lost and the child became a ward of the state. She remained a ward of the state from the time she was two years old until she was probably around 14 years old. When the girl was 14, allegations of sexual abuse rose, causing her to be removed from her foster home. Since her biological mother had been clean for several years, rather than place the girl in a new foster home she was placed back in the home with the mother. Seemed like a great idea. The problem was that the mother did not have to participate in any parenting classes or any kind of specialized training in order to prove that she had developed the parenting skills and was ready to be a mother again. So, quite naturally, the mother and daughter struggled to get along, causing the girl to have problems in school, which is how the young lady ended up in our program.

Initially, we were making tremendous progress with the young lady. However, for some reason the mother seemed to block all of our efforts. When we scheduled trainings for life skills, the mother would not let the daughter attend. When we found a therapist to provide one-on-one counseling, the mother said that she would find her own counselor. When we recommended a program that would offer social and emotional support, the mother said she had her own support system. So, the mother fought all of our efforts to help her child, but the child still clung to her mentor. I am sure this must have created some envy and jealousy for the mother towards the mentor. The turning point came when the mother called the mentor on the phone one day and said, with the child in the room with her, "didn't you tell me that _____ left school early today and should have been home by 3:00." The mentor was outdone because she had talked to neither the mother nor the daughter that day. Sure enough, when she got to the school the next day, the daughter told her mentor not to say anything to her and wanted to hear no explanation. So, even though the trust had not been violated, the fact that the young lady thought it had been violated was enough to shut down the relationship. The young lady went on to have major difficulties in school and refused to work with us again. Since that experience, I have often wondered if maybe we had not done enough to secure the confidence of the mother. Maybe if we had been more clear and transparent in our communication with the parent, and had a better understanding of her expectations of us we may have been able to prevent that situation from happening.

Lesson Three: The power of transparency

The third major lesson and the most important in developing relationships with the parents is recognizing the power of transparency. One of the ways to help in the parent/mentor relationship is by being transparent.

Honesty with the parents, even during difficult subjects will go a long way in establishing that necessary trust. One of our students had a troubled relationship with his mother. The child was working an internship with our office that paid him something like $200 a week. We got the child the internship because in spite of good grades and a warm personality, he had poor appearance, and found it difficult to make friends. We believed that if he could improve his outer appearance that he would begin to feel better about himself and his self-esteem would be enhanced. The child believed the mother was on drugs and would take his money, so he did not want her to know about the internship. So, we did not tell her. However, when he went shopping and came into the house with new clothes, she inquired about it until he had to tell her that he had the internship. Needless to say, she was extremely angry with us for withholding that information. So, when she called the office to discuss this, she was not using her inside voice. The first thing I did was ask her if it was okay to come by and discuss this in person. After a few more obscenities, she agreed. When we sat down, I did not respond to her anger, I did not let her see my anger, nor did I lie about withholding information. Instead, I accepted responsibility.

I told her that we had identified low self-esteem as the major issue causing her son the problems he was experiencing. We therefore thought that if he could improve his wardrobe and hygiene that it would do wonders towards improving his behavior, which is why we set him up with the internship. However, because I was concerned about whether or not he would get to keep the money long enough to do something nice for himself, I thought it best that we forego some of the usual formalities so that he could get immediate assistance. She was not satisfied. "I did not sign anything so how is he able to work without my consent?" I reminded her that she had given her consent when he first came into the program. On a side note, we will discuss documentation in a later chapter, but it is most important to have clearly defined policies governing your program, and all staff should have familiarity with these policies. I actually showed her the consent form, and reassured her that I was only trying to do all I could to help her son. She still was not happy, but at least she was no longer angry. I saw it as progress and felt pretty good about things after I left. Two weeks later, after he had gotten a fresh haircut, and purchased school clothes and shoes from his second check, she called again. This time she called to thank me. She said that she was grateful that she would not have to worry about school clothes for him so she could focus on the other children. Had we not been honest with her, we would have never had such a breakthrough.

Later, when our funding was cut, this parent was one of the parents who wrote a letter expressing her unhappiness with the program's funding being cut. Our transparency concerning her son shed light on how the program worked, so she then understood the direct connection between the funding, and the internship that helped her son so she became an advocate for the program. The son understood his mother's lack of financial support as an economic condition, rather than a lack of love for him. He learned that she was not on drugs, but in fact had to take care of him and his younger siblings by herself which is why she was not always able to provide for him. Through our ability to be transparent with the parent and child, they were able to be transparent with each other, and as a result, our relationship with the parent was improved, but more importantly, the relationship between the child and the parent improved as well.

Lesson Four: Safety First

The fourth lesson in developing relationships with parents is realizing they want to know their children are safe when they are with you. A parent is assuming that when you pick their child up from home or school, that they are safe while they are in your custody, and you will return them the same way you took them. Background checks offer parents assurance that the people who are working with their children have clean records and therefore pose no known dangers to their children. While these background checks in no way ensure nothing will happen, they do show parents that the organization is taking precautionary measures to make sure that the children are not exposed to adults who will harm them. However, they do not ensure safety.

One of the best ways I found to make parents feel as though I was offering a safe environment for their children was by allowing them to see and get to know me beyond my administrative role. I am a husband, and father of three, and I intentionally keep my family close by any program that I work with. I do this for a couple of reasons. One reason I do it is because I never want my children to resent the children I work with, or feel like I spend more time with those children than I do with my own. So, I bring my children with me so that they know they are important to me, but also so they can get to know the children I work with. This has resulted in my children developing friendships that last to this day with many of the children from my programs. However, one of the primary reasons I bring my children around is so that the parents of the children I work with can see how I interact with my own children. Therefore, when I pick up their children and tell the parents that I will care for their child as if they were my very own, there is actually a point of reference for them. They have seen how I treat my own, and that makes them feel as though I will keep their children safe as well.

Youth workers who are new, or do not have children of their own can still create an environment of safety for their parents. Acknowledging the parents' concerns prior to beginning to work with their children is one way a safe environment can be created. I remember a young lady who was in one of my programs developing an affinity for me. The young lady grew up in a single family home, and clearly (to me it was clear) she looked to me as the father figure who was missing out of her life. However, because she *always* wanted to be with me, and never wanted to stay in programs, one of my female staff members thought that this young lady's attraction to me bordered on impropriety. I did not agree, however it brought to my attention the possibility of impropriety, and it was that possibility that I had in mind when I decided to request a conference with the parent. I told the parent everything. I told her of the observations and concerns of my female staff member; we discussed her never wanting to go to programs; and we discussed the child's absentee father, and the impact his absence had on her daughter. At the end of this discussion the mother told me that she felt like a load had been lifted off of her back. She said she wanted to provide a strong male presence for her daughter, but was skeptical of bringing men around her, in fear of her mature development. She said that she knew her daughter had bonded with me, and wanted to approach me to discuss all of this, but was not comfortable enough to approach me. Acknowledging her concern, and being open and transparent allowed us to connect, and as a result of the mother's support, her daughter and I remain close to this day. She is in college, and doing well, because her parent, and mentor came together early on in the relationship and identified how the mentor could best help the young lady. Not only did we dispel the notion that a female student needed a female mentor, but coming together in a way that was transparent and honest allowed the parent to develop enough trust that her daughter would be safe. The parent's comfort allowed me the opportunity to provide for the student exactly what she needed from our relationship, and as a result the young lady blossomed.

Developing Positive Relationships within the School

A major stumbling block that can occur when working with students with troubled pasts lies in the development of the relationship between the mentor and the faculty and staff at the school the students attend. As mentors when we get a student, we are excited about the opportunity of working with a new student. We think of the fun we will have and the impact we can make on the new student. While the school on the other hand, looks at the same student and are reminded of the many times that same student had disrupted the learning process for other students. Initially the school and the mentor will probably be operating from differing points of view as to how these particular students can best be served.

We had a student who was the leader in a girl gang at the school. She was 19 years old, and had accumulated less than 10 hours in her 4 years in the school. When I took her and her mother to the school to withdraw her from the school the security guard that let us into the building did not let us out of her sight. I am sure that the security guard was thinking about all of the problems this young lady had caused during her time at the school. However, because we had no prior history to hold against her we were able to be non-judgmental in our relationship with the student. In all honesty, the real challenge for us was to avoid judging the school. We felt as though the school system, even if not our particular school was at fault for the condition in which we found the students. We repeatedly saw instances of students' rights being violated, and students being targeted, provoked, and even ridiculed by faculty and staff who were being paid to educate and protect them. This young woman being treated like a criminal was only one example.

There was one instance where a young man was told by security that he was being sent home and could not return until he brought a parent with him. The young man, of course not knowing any better and wanting to avoid further trouble, did as he was told, and left the school without a parent being called, the first violation of his rights. However, the next day he returned to school, late, and without a parent. We knew he would return without a parent because we knew this young man well and knew that he did not have a responsible adult who would attend on his behalf. When the young man showed up to school he was confronted by a security guard who told him that he was not allowed in the building without his parents. However, before his rights could be violated again, one of the mentors told the security guard that legally the young man could not be sent home without contacting his parents. When the school called the student's home they got no answer and were forced to let him stay. So, rather than letting the student go to class, the school decided to make the student go to In-School Suspension instead. The security guard who had stopped the student at the door was the same one who escorted him to the In-School Suspension room. The security guard proceeded to berate the young man during the entire walk to the In-School Suspension room. The security guard called the young man stupid, and told him he would never amount to anything, called him a loser, and hurled countless other insults at him, the second violation of his rights, humiliating him instead of helping him. By the time they reached the In-School Suspension room the young man was steaming mad. He was so angry that he stood at the garbage can and talked to himself while peeling an orange. Instead of giving the young man his space to heal, the security guard in the room preferred to listen to what the young man was saying to himself and then proceeded to call the first security guard to inform him of what the young man said he would do to him. Instead of the first security guard chalking these comments up to the ramblings of a troubled young man, who might I mention was taking medication for ADHD, he decided to come up to the room to confront the young man. When the security guard arrived, he got in the young man's face while the other security guard laughed, and sat there and did nothing to stop him, a third violation of the student's rights, as the security guards are actually paid to protect the children. The student responded by promptly mopping the floor with the security guard. The student was subsequently disciplined by being expelled from school while the security guard took a couple days off work to let his wounds heal and was then right back on the job.

As we frequently saw these kinds of abuses of power, and violations of students' rights it was difficult not to judge the school for allowing them. However, instead of judging, we learned valuable lessons from observing these inconsistencies.

Lesson One: The School is NOT the enemy

The first major lesson in developing positive relationships with the school is recognizing that the school deserves the same level of understanding that I am proposing be given to the students and their parents. When looked at honestly, one cannot ignore the reality that schools are under an extraordinary amount of stress. This was especially true in Chicago where the many children being killed laid unfair blame at the doors of Chicago Public Schools. In addition to the variety of violence plagued social issues that schools have to contend is the real challenge of educating students who are not prepared. Teachers and schools are judged on how well their students perform on statewide standardized exams. How is this judgment an accurate measure when teachers who are supposed to teach Algebra, Geometry, and Biology are getting students who are reading on second and third grade levels and can barely add and subtract in some cases? This challenge accompanied by the often disrespectful and unappreciated way teachers and principals are handled by both school administrators and parents make the challenges faced by school staffs very real. On top of all of this, schools are charged with protecting thousands of students on a daily basis, while the social issues being faced by these students go ignored, and the blame is again laid at the feet of the schools when incidents happen. Budget cuts tie principals' hands, making necessities like nurses, therapists, tutors, social workers, and reading specialists impossible to keep on staff as often as they are needed. Oftentimes, schools are forced to offer these kinds of services on a weekly basis when the reality is that their services are needed daily. As a result, I guess students have to wait until the day the nurse is in before they can get sick. This is ridiculous, and puts principals in an extremely unfair position when it comes to the safety of their students. There is no way that as a mentoring agency we could go into a school, see all of these dynamics at work and not be empathetic to the schools.

Lesson Two: good people work in the schools

The second lesson in working with the schools is recognizing that there are good people in the schools who want to help and you have to find those people. Principals, teachers, engineers, and even the staff members who work in the Attendance and Counseling Offices can be extremely helpful, and developing relationships with them all will make your life easier, and can enhance your ability to help the children. They can provide:

Attendance Data: This data will help you evaluate trends to identify truancy issues. In one school we were able to improve a student's attendance by simply buying him an alarm clock, and another student we improved their attendance by providing bus passes. With both of these students we identified their issues by studying the attendance trends we saw in the data we got from the Attendance Office.

Student Transcripts: From the transcripts you can follow your students' academic progress and identify the kinds of support they need. In one instance, we helped identify a class that a student who was a senior was missing that the student needed to graduate. The student's counselor had missed this and had we not caught it the student would not have found out he was missing the class until it was too late and he would not have graduated. Other students who were on course to graduate when they were 20 and 21 years old we were able to get into Alternative Schools where they instead graduated with their class based on the information we obtained from their transcripts, which we received from their counselors.

Parent/Student Portals: Access to the portals allows you to monitor how your students are performing in each class. You will be able to check on a weekly basis to see if your students are cutting classes, missing assignments, or failing exams, information that will go a long way in creating a way for you to keep your students accountable. Access to the portals is information you can get from the school Counseling Office.

Special perks: In addition to the copies of transcripts and attendance data they provide, and access to the portals, when the relationships are really good the office staff can help you in a number of other ways. I have had school office staff that would make copies for me of permission slips and other documents I needed to send home or give to the students. I have had office staff members make announcements during home room of information I needed to get out to the students in a hurry. I even had an office member allow me to use their personal computer when my internet was down.

Over the years through my career I have had great relationships with the schools my students have attended, which I attribute to a large part of the success my programs have enjoyed. My ability to develop great relationships with the schools was because I was able to convince them that I was genuinely there to help the children. They knew from the passion in which I advocated on their behalf, that I loved the kids. In spite of the bureaucracy that schools can become, many of the staff still work in the school because they too love the kids. The staff members who are there because they love the kids will want to help you based on a shared love of the children.

However, even if the staff members who work in the office are not cooperative, which is certainly sometimes the case, there are still things you can do to help develop the relationship and get them to want to help you.

Lesson Three: Be considerate

The third lesson in working with the schools is consideration. As mentioned previously school personnel endure a lot of stress, with principals and teachers often being judged by unfair performance measures. However, administrative assistants, and office staff who work in schools are often under just as much stress as the teachers and principals, if not more. The office staff: are often overworked and underpaid; endure the daily outbursts of irate parents; deliver disciplinary measures to students, and provide support for stressed out principals. With this in mind, as a mentor attempting to work with a school there are some things you can do to show your consideration for the support you are seeking.

Get parental consent: Before going to the office and requesting to see any attendance or academic documents from the students' files get parental consent first. This protects both you and the school. Parental consent makes it easy for the staff members that want to help you and gives you ammunition for the ones who may not want to help. The type of language that should be used in the Parental Consent form will vary from program to program, but make sure you include all of the necessary information you will need for reporting purposes, and to assist the students, i.e. access to report cards, attendance data, transcripts, etc.

Provide a list: Make the office aware of the students you work with in the school. Provide the office with a list of every student you work with in the school in addition to copies of the parental consent forms authorizing you to work with those students. Ask that the list be circulated among the teachers also. The list may change as you attract new students to your program. Each time new students are added provide the school with an updated roster of your students and consent forms for any students who have been added.

Be consistent in your request: Since you know the staff is busy, it will help to develop a consistent routine of your needs from the school. For example, if one of the things you want to monitor is student attendance data, you may want to develop a routine of making this request on Friday mornings for the attendance for the week. This will help the staff not feel overwhelmed by your request, and gives them an idea of how they can best assist you in your efforts to help your students.

Also make sure that there is only one designated person from your staff who makes request from the school. The school will appreciate and respect your efforts when there is order, and this includes having a recognized point person who makes requests and speaks on behalf of the program. When this level of consistency is in place the relationships will flourish. In two of the schools I worked the relationships were so good that I would get copies of my students report cards before the students or their parents even got them. In fact, in one of those schools the principal came into the school during her winter break just to print report cards for our program.

Bring your own supplies: Since you know that schools operate on tough budgets, particularly in poorer communities where the property taxes do not produce enough revenue to support the school's needs, bringing your own supplies allows the staff in the office to fulfill your requests at no additional cost to the school. I suggest bringing extra paper when you request transcripts or other items from your students' files. A little thoughtfulness goes a long way in establishing quality relationships within the school.

Show gratitude: Saying thank you, and showing gratitude when your requests are met shows the staff that you appreciate the time they spend honoring your requests. My staff and I would actually buy breakfast for the entire staff of the school a couple of times a year as a way of thanking the school staff for their support. We did not just do this for the principals and teachers, but for the entire staff of the school. It was no accident that we were able to get whatever we needed from the school, and were allowed to pretty much get access to anywhere in the school we needed to go. In fact in one school I was actually given keys and the alarm code and allowed to come and go as I pleased. Gratitude goes along way.

So, if your desire is to help the students in your program, establishing quality relationships with the students, parents, and schools will be integral in your ability to do so. The students themselves have a difficult time opening up to people. They have defense mechanisms built up that they have developed in order to protect themselves from a world they view as hostile and untrustworthy. You may be able to reach them on surface level topics, but you will not be able to penetrate the walls they have built up, without quality relationships. Parents and schools can be some of your greatest advocates or they can be some of your biggest adversaries in your efforts to do so. Which one, will be determined by the quality of the relationships you develop with them.

One of the messages I always stressed to my staff was that our first and primary objective was *always* to be an advocate for the student first. This means that we have to be prepared to defend the student's position against the parent when the parent is harming the child. We have to be willing to go against the teacher or the school when they might be harming the child. This does not mean that we fight the parent, or the school, but that we are effective mediators on behalf of our students. When we are most effective in our roles we will form a partnership with the parents and the school so that the child will have multiple adults advocating on their behalf. Positive relationships with the students, their parents, and the schools will create a major advantage in effectively mentoring "troubled" youth.

Chapter Four

The Power of Exposure

"We pay a price when we deprive children of exposure to the values, principles, and education they need to make them good citizens".
Sandra Day O'Connor

I remember being in church one Sunday morning and the preacher told a story about one of his political friends. According to the preacher, he and his political friend were planning a fishing trip. They had discussed fishing together before, but they were about to embark on their first fishing expedition together. When the preacher went to pick up the politician, the politician had on thigh high rubber boots, a rain coat and hat, and carried with him enough equipment to field a small army of professional fishermen. The preacher thought it a bit odd, but proceeded nonetheless towards his favorite fishing spot. The preacher said when he arrived at the fishing spot the politician took one look at the hole they were to fish in and began to die laughing. He said the politician laughed so hard that he was in tears and literally had to catch his breath. Once the politician finally stopped laughing, he had everyone reload the truck to drive to what was at the time an undisclosed location. Eventually, the preacher said they ended on a boat in the middle of a lake where they were fishing for 15 – 20 pound bass. The preacher said since that day he had yet to return to the watering hole. Once he had been exposed to something greater, he was unable to return to the hole from which he had once thought normal.

Robert Kiyosaki, in his famous book <u>Rich Dad Poor Dad</u> stated, "If a child is born to poor parents, the only thing the parents can teach the child is how to be poor." This is a simple statement, yet very profound when viewed through the lens of youth development. Taking that same concept and applying it to children who are: born to parents who lack social skills; or those raised by parents who undervalue or lack the ability to provide quality education; or those taught by parents with outdated concepts of child raising. What happens to these children? How can the parents teach skills that they themselves never learned? Like the analysis of being raised by the poor dad in Kiyosaki's book, the majority of these children will be raised in a manner that will almost ensure the same life and fate of the parents who raised them. However, this does not have to be the case. Mentors possess the power of the rich dad. Like the politician who introduced the idea of a bigger lake, mentors can present new ideas and information that can assuredly offer young people new perspectives on life.

There is tremendous evidence based support for the power of exposure. For example, in the case of the child being raised by the poor dad, through exposure to new ways of thinking about money an entirely new ideology about how money should be handled was created for the child. This new ideology created a paradigm shift that re-directed his entire financial future. Kiyosaki's words are not only profound, but his story bears witness to the truth of those words. As a result of the shift in thinking brought on by the rich dad, Kiyosaki went on to live a very rich, and profitable life. Likewise, children from dysfunctional families who are exposed to better values, principles, and education can have paradigm shifts that forever change the course of their lives.

A friend of mine was raising a daughter as an only child. My friend was married, although not to the daughter's father. The husband was a good man, and from a financial standpoint, provided a relatively good life for my friend and her daughter. While a good life was provided by the husband, he did not provide the kind of discipline and emotional support the girl needed for healthy development. As a result, when the girl turned 14 years old the mother started having problems with her. It started with small things like disobeying her mother's orders, and ignoring household chores. However, by the end of her freshman year, it turned into outright defiance with the girl staying out until the wee hours of the morning and returning smelling of alcohol. When grades came out at the end of her freshman year, the mother had seen enough. She called the biological father, who lived in another state at the time and told him about the trouble she was having with their daughter. The biological father suggested having the girl move with him. The mother resisted at first because the father lived in another state. However with the behavioral problems increasing the mother was at her wit's end and realized that something had to be done, as she feared she would lose her daughter to the streets.

Initially, the mother thought the girl would be kicking and screaming once she settled into her new home. However, the contrary proved to be true. It took the girl no time to settle in and make friends. In addition to making new friends, was the bonus that the friends she made were much different than the ones she had left behind. Her new friends happened to come from nice two parent families, where they were supported, and education and solid values were emphasized. This new influence brought about an instant change in the behavior of my friend's daughter. Her grades turned around instantly, and her behavior improved to the point that she became a positive role model for her peers. The truly amazing part of her story is that her transformation occurred, not over several years, but over the period of just one year. By the end of her first year in her new home, she began to attend church regularly. Her attitude improved, her grades improved, and she is now enrolled in college and doing well. As a result of this girl being *exposed* to a different way of living, she was given a chance to turn her life around, and she took advantage of it. The story of my friend's daughter story raises the question, how many others could change if they were actually given an opportunity to change?

Certainly not every child can be moved across the country. But like Sandra Day O'Connor said in the quote "when we deprive children of exposure we pay a price." All children can be exposed to art, culture, values, and other opportunities to expand and influence their thinking. Early on in the establishment of our mentoring program we took 25 children on a college tour of the universities in Illinois. Among the schools we visited were the University of Illinois in Champaign-Urbana, Western Illinois University in Macomb, IL, and Illinois State University in Normal, IL. We differed from most annual college tours in that we took non-traditional students with us. Among the students we took were first generation college students, students with learning and behavioral disabilities, and even students who had failed multiple classes at the high school level. One of our students, a 19 year old young lady had attended the school for 3 ½ years, and had only accumulated a total of 9 hours. She had been engaged in so many fights at the school that she was considered public enemy number 1 inside the school. We took her anyway, and as a result of being exposed to a different environment the light bulb went off for her. During that tour she was voted by our staff as the outstanding student participant of the college tour. The most rewarding moment for me, and the moment that assured me the bulb had went off for her was when she asked an admission counselor did she know the number of incoming freshmen that were accepted on an annual basis with a G.E.D. (General Equivalency Diploma) vs. the number that were accepted through traditional high school programs? When the counselor answered the question, and actually gave her the percentage that is allowed in annually with a G.E.D. I saw the light in her eyes. At that moment, she realized that college was a possibility.

This same student had another breakthrough at one of the hotels where we were staying during our tour. Another student came to my room to tell me that I needed to come to their room because her roommate was having a moment and she did not know what to do. When I got to their room, sure enough the young lady was crying and seemed to be having an emotional breakdown. When I asked her what was wrong, I was blown away by her response. "This is the first time anybody has ever cared about me. The first time anybody ever did something for me without expecting me to do something for them in return." (I failed to mention that the college tour was completely free for the 25 participants and they were allowed to eat whatever they wanted on the menu whenever we had meals.) She proceeded to tell me about her home life. She told me how she does not get a moment's rest at home. She said there were always people at her house. She said that her mom milked the welfare system and was encouraging her to do the same. She told me a story of how when she was 16 years old her mother told her that she should go out on the streets and do whatever she needed to do to earn some money. She told me stories of how her time spent with her biological father included him making statements dripping with sexual innuendoes, while looking at her in a manner that made her extremely uncomfortable. She told me how she told her mother, but her mother insisted she spend time with him anyway. She told me how she was violently raped by two of her cousins when she was 13 years old. One of the cousins would hold her down while the other would be on top of her, and when he was done they would switch positions. She told me how her mother did not believe her when she told her of the alleged sexual assault, and how it would go on every time they visited for the next several years before her older sister finally intervened to put a stop to it. Finally, she told me how she was grateful to go on the college tour because it gave her a chance to sleep in a normal bed. Needless to say, I was in tears by the time I was done talking to this young lady. However, not lost on me was the reality that had this girl not been selected to go on the college tour, this information may not have ever come out. It was through exposure to a different environment that caused this young lady to realize that something was wrong with the environment in which she lived. It was that realization that caused the emotional breakdown that opened the door to our ability to help her. Her honesty and forthrightness created a bond between her and I that exists to this very day. She remains in my estimation one of the most wonderful, loving, misunderstood students I have ever worked with, and will forever be one of my all-time favorites. Simply by exposing her to something different all kinds of possibilities opened up for us to help her.

Another example of the power of exposure can be seen in the students who completed training on etiquette we set up through The Etiquette Foundation of Illinois. Recognizing early on that the students lacked the social graces they would need for any long term success in mainstream society we sought the support of The Etiquette Foundation of Illinois. The Etiquette Foundation of Illinois has worked in several inner-city schools in Chicago and its surrounding community teaching etiquette to children of all ages. Etiquette sessions included:

- Developing Good Social Skills
- The Essence of Behavior, i.e., Manners, Comportment, Decorum, Courtesy etc.
- Building Confidence and Self-esteem
- Courtesy and Respect for Others
- The Role of Character and Personality as it Relates to Behavior
- Social Conduct and Image
- Appreciating The Arts and Humanities

- Table and Dining Etiquette

While some of these sessions may seem unnecessary, the truth of the matter is that they were completely necessary to re-program young people on how to publicly conduct themselves in an acceptable manner. Part of the stigma that follows young people today is that they do not know how to act. This was our initial thought, when we decided to set up the training. The evidence for the need for this type of training became completely clear once we began the workshops. Initially, the students were extremely loud and disrespectful towards the instructor, who literally had to raise his voice just to be heard by the few students who were paying attention. The instructor was never riled by the children's behavior, instead exhibiting great etiquette himself, and eventually winning the children over in the process. However, that is not what was most impressive about training the students in etiquette. The most valuable aspect of the etiquette program had to be the behavior demonstrated by the students who completed the training. Those students were clearly impacted by what they learned in that class, which was evident by the subsequent changes in their behavior.

When I think of the etiquette class, the student who comes to mind was a young man who was 17 years old and had developed a reputation of being a tough guy. A year prior, he had actually flipped a police officer at the school who he said had gotten too close to him. This young man was precisely the kind of kid we were told could not be helped. In fact he got into a verbal exchange with one of our mentors earlier in the year and he verbally assaulted the mentor for what he believed to be a show of disrespect. To put it mildly, this young man had an anger problem. We put him through a series of workshops on anger management, conflict resolution, and other life skills trainings. In addition to those workshops, he went through etiquette training.

After two weeks of sitting in the etiquette class, we began to notice a change. He would sit and closely listen to the instructor. One day while other students talked, we watched him concentrating on identifying the difference between the salad fork and the dinner fork. He was holding them both up and examining them closely. Clearly, understanding this difference had become important to him. By the end of the program, this young man had received a suit, matching shoes, a dress coat, and watch and was selected to go on the etiquette outing which included a sit down dinner at an exclusive Chicago restaurant, a cruise around Chicago, and a visit to the newly built Trump condominiums in Chicago, home to NBA all-star and Chicago native Derrick Rose. The young man was ecstatic, and since then has not looked back. He later went on a legal tour with the American Bar Association, where he tried a mock case, and did so well that he was offered a scholarship should he decide to pursue a legal career. Through exposure, positive values were learned that brought him immediate rewards but also that could have an extremely positive impact on the remainder of his life.

This young man was only one example of the power of exposure. Every student who completed our training on Etiquette experienced noticeable changes in their overall behavior. Several agencies around the country now plan annual college tours to provide the kind of exposure we provided in our tour of the schools in Illinois. The reason college tours are so effective is simple, they work. Exposure works! There is an old saying that goes, "you cannot miss what you have never had", but once you have had it…you know it is possible, and once you know excellence is possible, mediocrity becomes unacceptable.

.

Chapter Five

Documentation

"It does not matter if you have a child who wants to be an astronaut and you take him to the moon. If it is not documented, it did not happen"

Sidney W. Johnson

The quote for this particular chapter is one I have used often over the years. As I sought a quote that would place emphasis on the importance of documentation I found none better than the one I use for my own staff. In the world of grants, fundraisers, and private donations; and the land of lawsuits and allegations, nothing is more important than documentation. In an economy where philanthropic giving is on a decline, agencies struggle to make payroll, and dollars do not stretch as much as they once did, documentation is essential. One of the easiest things to do in the Not for Profit world is to get so engulfed in the good work one is doing that the process of documentation is not given the attention it deserves. Most people whom I have met during my years of working with children chose a career working with children because they were looking for a way to make the world a better place. I have NEVER in all of my years working with children met anyone who chose their career path because they thought they could get rich.

So, having said that, most of the people with whom I have come in contact have been much more focused on providing quality service than they have on proving that they are doing good work. These two dynamics, quality service vs. documentation do not appear to be contrary to one another, but oftentimes they can seem like they are. If I am a case manager who has ten students on my case load and their reports are due within the next couple of days. I will be spending all of my time finishing those reports. However, if one of the students on my case load is shot, or goes to prison, or is hospitalized, or has a family member hospitalized, most youth workers who are effective and compassionate about their students are going to leave the paperwork and go be with the one student who has experienced the tragedy. We would rather be there for one student during the time of crisis than to sit at home and write about what happened with the other nine students. So, in most cases, quality service will be selected over documentation when it comes down to developing priorities.

Documentation is often avoided because it is time consuming. In fact, writing case notes and reports can be extremely time consuming, especially when a case manager or youth worker has not developed a system that allows them to capture events in near Real Time. In other words, case notes and reports are much easier and much more effective when a log is used that documents events as they happen. Mentors should use a log that identifies:

- Student's name
- Date and Time of contact
- Method of contact, whether it was phone, e-mail, or in person
- Who was present during interaction

- Duration of the contact
- Issues that were discussed
- Recommendations that were suggested

This log will allow the mentor to jot down information as it happens so that case notes and reports become a matter of simply transferring information from one document to another. Also, the logs themselves can be bound in individual files for each student that can serve as additional documentation. When logs are not used, mentors and case managers are often forced to attempt to recall dates and conversations that are remembered neither accurately nor completely and valuable information is often lost. The primary problem with case notes is that they can become a drag to do and their importance is often overshadowed by the work itself.

However, as understandable as the arguments against documentation goes, the truth of the matter is that documentation is a necessity that there is just no way around. Even with modern technology allowing real time scanning, and computer software having the ability to capture, store, and track information on each individual student and their progress; proper documentation should still be the primary management tool used in demonstrating the effectiveness of your program, and the impact being made on your students.

Documentation is important and deserves attention for three very important reasons:

1. *Documentation provides evidence based support that your program works.*

2. *Documentation allows an observer to recognize patterns and trends with individual youth, and the program itself,*
3. *Documentation tells your story in a way that you never could without it.*

Why Evidence Based Supportive Practices?

The first and in my opinion, the primary reason for documentation is to provide evidence based support for your program. Evidence-based practice refers to the use of interventions, strategies, programs and supports that have research documenting their effectiveness. As was mentioned earlier the decline in philanthropic giving, and the economic recession have caused competition for grants, and fundraising to grow tremendously over the past several years. Those who employ programs with evidence based support are at a distinct advantage for finding funding sources for obvious reasons. People who can afford to support programs want to make sure the programs that they support work. Quite simply, federal and state sponsoring agencies, as well as private donors want accountability from programs and wish to see results from their investments. In order for a program to be called "evidence-based," the following things must happen:

- Evaluation research must show that the program produced positive results.
- The results produced can be attributed to the program itself, rather than to other extraneous factors or events.
- The evaluation is peer-reviewed and supported by experts in the field; and

- The program is "endorsed" by a federal agency or respected research organization and included in their list of effective programs.

The criteria given for evidence based programming offers a sound explanation as to why evidence based programs work. Programs with evidence based support have been researched, other contributing factors have been considered, experts in the field have signed their seal of approval, and federal or state agencies have endorsed that they work. This also explains why donors would rather support your program when it is designed around evidence based practices. Instead of placing resources into program development, it is logical for those with resources to place those resources into programs that have demonstrated an ability to work. Documenting your efforts allows you to align your program's strengths with those programs more likely to be funded.

However, one of the challenges presented through the use of evidence based programs is that even though they have been researched and have demonstrated an ability to work, they are not a guarantee for success. For example, a program may have evidenced based support that it works well in preventing gang activity in Chicago. Someone works with youth and has identified the need for a gang prevention program in Los Angeles. The program in Chicago will provide a framework that may allow for success if implemented in Los Angeles, but there is no guarantee. A factor such as the relationship between the gangs and the individuals implementing the program in Chicago may have contributed to the success of the Chicago program, and may be a luxury the individuals implementing the program in Los Angeles do not enjoy. If the relationships between the gangs in L.A. and the individuals implementing the program are not as solid as the relationships in Chicago, then the program in L.A. may not work even though it is evidence based on a program in Chicago that worked.

Another challenge that one attempting to use a mentoring program with evidence based support is that there may be very limited evidence based support for the kind of program being implemented. If a program is innovative, or targeted to a specific audience there may not be enough information available to find support. This situation is especially common when it comes to the promotion of positive outcomes rather than the prevention of negative ones. Because the development of many evidence based programs was sponsored by federal and state agencies concerned with addressing specific problems, such as substance abuse, mental illness, violence, or delinquency, there currently exist many more problem-focused evidence based programs than ones designed specifically to promote positive developmental outcomes. If I have an idea to use rap music to teach reading to students who struggle with literacy. My program may be exactly the innovative idea that this population of student needs to learn to read. However, I will run into problems trying to identify evidence based support for such a program. In this instance I would attempt to build my support around other programs that have demonstrated the ability to use music as a tool to teach non-music related subjects.

Finally, a major challenge in using evidence based programs is finding the financial resources needed to adopt and implement them. Most evidence based programs are developed, copyrighted, and sold at rather substantial costs. Program designers often require that organizations purchase curricula and other specially developed program materials, the staff attend specialized training, and that program facilitators hold certain certifications. For organizations or individuals that lack financial independence, this can be quite challenging. Documenting your program prepares you to meet that challenge.

However, in spite of the challenges presented by evidence based programs, they still remain an effective tool for convincing potential funding sources of the viability of your program. One of the main reasons for this is because evidence based programs allow you to create realistic outcomes that are documented to demonstrate the effectiveness of your program. Outcomes should be the driving force for your mentoring program. What do you expect to see from the students in your program? Outcomes allow you to: impress funders, identify what is and is not working, and keep your students motivated. The desired outcomes should be developed from the program's goals and objectives, and should be measurable.

In the movie the Karate Kid, a young man had relocated to a new town where he is subsequently harassed by bullies who know karate and use it to beat the young man up pretty regularly. However, the young man is fortunate and meets a neighbor who feels sorry for him and agrees to teach him karate. They begin to meet on a pretty consistent basis, but the young man notices that all of his lessons seem to help the neighbor more than they are helping him. The neighbor has the young man paint his fence and house, wax his many cars, and sand his wooden floors. After doing this kind of labor for a while, the young man gets angry and confronts the neighbor whom he thinks is making a fool out of him at this point. The young man insists that the neighbor has been using him, has taught him nothing and as a result, refuses to do anything else the neighbor suggests. Meanwhile, the neighbor insists that the boy has learned plenty of karate, and is merely looking at things the wrong way. So, the neighbor asks the boy to do one of the chores he had been doing, i.e. paint the fence. The boy refuses at first because he is angry at his perceived deception. However, he relents and begins to do it. Once the boy begins to do the motions for the labor he had been given, i.e. paint the fence, wax the car, sand the floors; the neighbor shows him how those same motions translate into karate moves. So, while the boy does the motions of labor, the neighbor shows him how to use those same motions for karate….and the boy gets it. It wasn't enough for the neighbor to tell the young man he had learned plenty. But, allowing the young man to see what he had learned motivated him in a way that the neighbor never could have done with his words. This is the power of outcomes. They tell the story that your words cannot tell, and evidence based programs provide solid examples of demonstrated outcomes.

Tell Your Story

One of the challenges that most bothered me in trying to run a successful mentoring program was the emphasis placed on quantitative data. If the program is geared towards addressing school related issues, the benchmarks may include: increase in attendance; reduction in out-of-school suspensions; and an improvement in academic performance, or some similar set of outcomes. This data is actually a great tool to determine the effectiveness of your program. However, it should not be the only criteria used in determining your program's effectiveness. Equally important is the qualitative data which is not as easily measured, but just as important in determining if the program works. Documentation allows you to tell the qualitative story of your program's success that may get missed when looking at numbers.

We had a young lady who was an 18 year old sophomore when she entered our program. She had earned less than 10 credit hours during the four years she had been in high school. The first thing we did when we got her on our caseload was to test her. We found that she was reading on a second grade level. We then set her up with a reading specialist who worked with her 3 to 4 times a week for a minimum of 30 minutes per session. While her reading began to improve almost immediately, she was so far behind that she still struggled to improve her academic performance in school. Eventually, we realized that this young lady would be better off in an alternative setting where she could get the kind of personal assistance she needed. We discussed this with her mother who agreed with our assessment and enrolled her in an alternative program. Once in that setting, this young lady began to excel in a way that none of us had imagined she could. She graduated from the alternative school and is now enrolled in junior college. However, at the time our program was being evaluated, she would have been seen as a negative hit against the program because she did not demonstrate improvement in the areas of focus. This is a major benefit of documentation. It allows you to tell a part of the story that cannot be told through simply looking at the numbers. It is an equally important part of the story, but less measurable and therefore more difficult to see when evaluating the success of a program. Qualitative data is captured in the case notes that should be completed on a weekly basis. Once the information is gathered from the mentors or case managers, it should be placed in a narrative that accompanies whatever data has to be submitted as part of the program's reporting requirements.

Case Notes

Case notes are extremely important when working with children. Case notes:

- Record important details about services provided.
- Supplement and synthesize information on a young person's strengths and needs in a range of areas to provide a justification for specific services and activities provided.

- Serve as documentation of factors affecting a young person's eligibility or other important information.
- Record details of a young person's participation in activities and progress toward his or her employment and educational goals.

Case notes do not just repeat information gathered during intake and initial assessment. Rather, they provide an explanation of how planned activities addressed the specific issues and barriers that were identified during that information gathering session. In simple terms, case notes describe how each activity will build on the young person's strengths and address the barriers preventing them from achieving their desired goals. In addition, case notes are sometimes allowed as acceptable documentation for eligibility factors to verify low income status, or in court proceedings to demonstrate a child's efforts to turn around previously undesirable behavior. Case notes should begin immediately after a student has been accepted into the program, and should be done regularly for every participant in the program. In addition, case notes should include:

- Date of the conversation or activity being documented.
- Name of the staff person documenting the information, and their relation to the student, i.e. mentor, project manager, etc.
- Details of the conversation/activity that took place, i.e. the student played well with others, student had a verbal exchange with another

student, student revealed he is not eating dinner because no food is available, etc.

- The goals that were set during the conversation/activity.
- Any supportive services offered during the conversation, even if the services offered were refused.
- Purpose of the discussion/activity as it relates to the student's overall goals set during the assessment.

It is important when doing case notes to remember that case notes are legal documents that should identify services being provided, and set goals for future progress. Case notes are legal documents representing you, your agency, and the student. So, accuracy when doing case notes should be your focal point. In order to better ensure accuracy in your case notes:

- Record facts only – behaviors you observed and statements you heard; do not attempt to make a diagnosis.
- Record facts accurately and completely.
- Avoid judgmental opinions, stereotypical comments, or any offensive statements i.e. the student's behavior was bad.
- Do not make any comment you could not defend or prove in a court of law, i.e. the student is being abused. Unless you have documentation verifying that abuse was found, the student made allegations of abuse.

- If you must state an opinion relevant to the youth's participation and progress, be sure to label your statement as an opinion.
- Use clear, simple, concise language, including professional terminology when appropriate, avoiding the use of slang, street language, clichés, jargon, and other sarcastic comments.
- Avoid metaphors or similes; just say what you mean directly. (you are writing case notes, not a work of fiction)
- Do not comment on details that are not relevant to the youth's progress

Think of the case notes as an accurate depiction of your student's life. Whether the case notes are reviewed by a co-worker, school administrator, counselor, or judge. Whomever it is that views the notes, you want to give them an accurate reflection of that student, and a clear picture of what the student has been exposed to since entering the program.

Even though documentation can be time consuming and a drag to do, remember the big picture. Solid documentation serves your students immeasurably by allowing you to:

- Maximize outcomes.
- Remain consistent with changes and developments.
- Provide data to respond to accountability demands of funders and grantors.
- Expand the skills and competence of your students.

- Enhance opportunities to solicit additional support for your program
- Provide rationale for the continued need for the services you are providing.
- Tell your story.

So, whether you are a trained professional mentor, or just mentoring a kid who lives on your block, take a few minutes daily to document your efforts. While documentation may not be the most rewarding aspect of working with children, it certainly is one of the most important aspects. Keep this in mind when doing them.

Chapter Six

The Model for Success

"The greatest good you can do for another is not just to share your riches but to reveal to him his own."
Benjamin Disraeli

One of the greatest obstacles one faces when choosing a career of service is the feeling that the work they are doing is in vain. Because of the nature of this line of work, oftentimes the impact that is being made goes unseen by the one who is making it. Many times mentors, teachers, youth workers, and other caring adults plant seeds in the minds and hearts of young people that will not take root until years after the young person has left their presence. Just as Mrs. Thompson did not see the long term effect that her words would have on me. Those of us who work with young people have to understand this and therefore cannot get sidetracked by taking it personally when we do not see immediate progress in our students. Oftentimes, we may see no progress at all, but that does not mean we are not making an impact. Because we live in the "grant dependent world" defined by the burdens of refunding, benchmarks, and deliverables, we often place unrealistic expectations on ourselves, our programs, and the students we serve.

On the one hand, we need to meet the deliverables in order to continue running our program. However, on the other hand, we are faced with the reality that we know many of our students are not ready for the strides our programs demand of them. This dilemma led me to several questions: "Why does mentoring seem to work for some students, but not for others? What is wrong with the students who are not being helped? Is help available for those students? And, are we not working hard enough to help those students?" Many years of doing this work and pondering over these questions, led me to a realization. I realized that the progress or lack of progress we saw in our students had little to do with our program. I mean sure, the quality of the program itself is necessary to ensure any opportunities for growth for the program's participants. However, I realized that the rate at which a child develops in the program or in life was based on several factors that had little to do with the program and its staff. The following questions came to mind and I discovered that in their answers laid the solution to our dilemma. Does the child want to change? How deep and what are the issues causing the misbehavior? Are the resources available to help the child deal with the issues causing the misbehavior? This analysis led me to the following formula, which I believe is the model for mentoring troubled youth, and provides them with the greatest opportunity for growth and impact.

*The Rate of Recovery = Depths of the Issues * Desire to Change * Access to Resources*

Following this model allowed us to individualize service plans for each student that was in direct correlation with that student's individual needs. This model also limited our levels of frustration, as we did not force our expectations onto our students, understanding that how soon the student improved was dependent upon a host of variables, and was not a reflection on us and our program.

Depths of the Issues

More times than not, when we follow this model the only role we play when there seems to be lack of progress with a child is that we underestimate the depths of the issues, or are limited in our access to the resources needed. Deep issues may not be limited to poor communities, and personal issues are certainly not limited by race, gender, or socio-economic status. However, as we have discussed in previous chapters, the damage that has been done to many who grew up in poorer communities, has caused a variety of mental health issues, loss of self-esteem, identity struggles, and inferiority complexes.

In the book, 'The Wretched of the Earth' Algerian psychiatrist Franz Fanon discusses people who survived the violent Algerian revolution. He states that victims of torture experienced everything from extreme paranoia to psychosomatic illnesses. Many African Americans have also been victims of torture and like the survivors of the Algerian revolution may be prone to struggles with extreme paranoia and psychosomatic illnesses. Many within the African American community and the country at large will disagree, as on the surface this seems to be quite an extreme comparison. After all, the Algerian revolution consisted of an indiscriminate policy of torture, murder and abuse that would make the African-American struggle seem mild in comparison. But stopping the comparison before taking a more thorough look at the similarities would be a mistake. When making this comparison, consider: the lynching of African American fathers and husbands and the fear these lynchings must have caused to exist in African American families; the Jim Crow laws, and the humiliation that they must have caused to parents who had to explain to their children why they had to drink from dirty, unsanitary fountains; the separation of families, and the distrust and disconnect that must have been created within the community; the forced religious conversions, and the loss of identity that must have accompanied them; the rapes, and loss of dignity, self-respect, and humiliation that its victims must have felt; the blatant legal disregard shown in cases like 'Brown vs. the Board of Education' and 'Plessy vs. Ferguson', the murders of African American leaders like Martin Luther King, Jr., Malcolm X, and Medgar Evers; and countless other experiences unique to the African-American experience make this comparison very real. When the unique experiences of African-Americans are examined as it relates to the psychological damage brought on by these experiences are combined with the often undiagnosed and untreated individual traumas many have experienced, the comparison of extreme paranoia and psychosomatic illnesses experienced in Algeria seems a relatively simple and easy comparison to make. Ask 100 African American men what they are feeling when a police officer is behind him, and if they are honest, the majority will say fear. The fear having been brought on by the unique experiences of African American men with law enforcement. African American criminals are not the only ones who feel this fear. Many African American men who are educated and familiar with the Rodney king beating, the Henry Louis Gates situation, the Trayvon Martin murder, and similar such cases will tell you that they feel the same fear. This fear of police officers, and authority figures in general is often intensified in African American youth, masked by tough exteriors and sagging pants.

Especially disturbing about the paranoia and fear is the reality that no one seems to care, or want to talk about fixing the problems that have created it. When African Americans attempt to discuss the damages brought on by slavery and Jim Crow the response is always something like "that was a long time ago, get over it," preventing honest dialogue from happening. The lack of dialogue creates a sense of hopelessness that makes young people especially susceptible to crime. With no family in place to provide nurturing, direction, or guidance, many turn to the streets and become menaces to society.

In Sociology, what I have explained as the reality of the African American experience would be defined as internalized social oppression. Internalized social oppression is the manner in which an oppressed group comes to use against itself the methods of the oppressor. Carter G. Woodson explained in 'The Mis-Education of the Negro'

"If you can control a man's thinking you do not have to worry about his action. When you determine what a man shall think you do not have to concern yourself about what he will do. If you make a man feel that he is inferior, you do not have to compel him to accept an inferior status, for he will seek it himself. If you make a man think that he is justly an outcast, you do not have to order him to the back door. He will go without being told; and if there is no back door, his very nature will demand one."

Carter G. Woodson explained in this passage the very issue that today demands a formula to overcome. This issue may be considered taboo or playing the race card by some, but Kiyosaki identified what happens when wrong thinking is not corrected.

Some Latinos also have a challenge in this area as they too have challenges unique to their community. An example would be a Latino child born in the United States with a parent who is facing deportation, and another working to make ends meet. The anxiety and fear that would be created in this situation would more than likely be internalized by that child. Whether the parent is later deported or not is irrelevant because the fear that was created is real in the mind of the child. The parent struggling to provide will undoubtedly be burdened with stress, and as a result will further the fear, anxiety, and powerlessness which has already been planted. When that child gets older and challenges and obstacles in life occur, unless the child has been provided coping tools to help him, fear will govern how the child responds to those challenges, making life difficult.

Internalized social oppression is not limited to African-Americans or Latinos, or any other minority group for that matter. Nonetheless, due to the unique experiences of these groups, as well as some of the previously mentioned issues, it is certainly easy to see how internalized social oppression has come to exist in these groups, and why some innovative, transparent, and authentic ways of looking at these issues are necessary in order for any real progress to be made.

I was watching a video on YouTube in which someone was doing a demonstration on the power of the mind and they used an example of eating bad food. If someone were to eat a steak that made them sick to the point that they had to be hospitalized for food poisoning; every time that person sees, thinks about, or is presented a steak to eat that looks like the particular steak that made them sick, they may experience nausea and may actually get sick all over again. This is an example almost everyone has experienced at some point in his or her life. Even though we know realistically that a steak we ate years ago cannot make us sick today, the mind, in an effort to protect us from getting sick again will convince us that it can. The students we work with have been using "mean mugs", "cold stares", fighting, intimidation, cursing and swearing, and other negative behaviors to protect themselves from adults, predatory bullies, life situations, and other things that have caused them harm for as far back as they can probably remember. This behavior, (defense mechanisms) that serves their best interest by protecting them from predators when they are young makes them menaces to society, and gets them prison sentences when they get older. And even when this has been explained to students over and over again, the fear they have internalized causes them to function in a manner contrary to their own best interest.

Plato emphasized this same point in his "Myth of the Cave". Plato said, if one were to take a prisoner captive, and chain him inside a cave facing the wall. The only thing the captive would be able to see are the shadows that appear on the wall of the people walking behind him. Plato argued that if the captive was caused to stay in that condition for so long, he would come to accept those shadows as reality. Plato went on to say that if you freed the captive after having kept him on the wall for so long, and the captive was faced with real people, the captive would be afraid and unable to adjust. His mind having become adapted to the shadows on the wall. Many young people have been living in sub-standard living conditions for so long that the thought of anything better is unrealistic to them. Understanding the depths of the issues affecting them is paramount in a mentor's ability to help a child.

I was out with my son one day when I got into an argument with a man in a parking lot. My son was 16 years old at the time. I started out trying to reason with the other gentleman. He called me all kinds of names and hurled a bunch of insults and obscenities my way. Initially I continued to try and talk with him, but clearly he did not want to reason. I consider myself to be one of the more conscious, loving people around. I am very aware socially and emotionally of how my behavior affects other people. I am also very aware of how life pushes even the nicest people to the edge sometimes. So, it is extremely possible that the guy with whom I was ready to fight was not a bad guy at all. In fact, he could have been a very nice man who was just having a bad day and who I just so happened to meet at the wrong time. So, even though I knew that the man was probably dealing with some of the same frustration that gets me sidetracked at times, the truth is at that moment it did not matter. I was ready to pull my car over, get out of the car, and go blow for blow with a man that was at least my age, and with whom I had never seen, nor had any prior contact.

Even adults with years of accomplishments, great insight, and track records of success can be affected by their issues and make bad decisions. My son said, "Dad you are a respected member of society, that man is not on your level and you cannot let him pull you down to his level. He is the type of person you work every day to try and help." My sixteen year old son had to remind me of the message I give to kids every day. Then, even after hearing him say it, I still struggled to calm down. A part of me wanted to finish the confrontation, but I had tools to combat that part of me, and thankfully, after years of self-help, including finding a spiritual practice that works for me, and several wonderful people whom God has placed on my life path, I had begun to heal enough to allow my cooler head to prevail. My prayer is that this work will encourage someone else so that as a result of this work, others may begin to heal also, and children will get the help they need to have a chance at life. Twenty years ago, if I had gotten into such an argument, someone might have said the same things my son said to me, and it might have fallen on deaf ears. But because I knew the depths of my issues, and constantly possessed a strong desire and determination to change, people came along at just the right times to provide the resources that gave me the tools I needed to have an opportunity to change.

Desire to Change

Desire to change will be the most difficult part of the formula to measure. In fact, it is probably an element that cannot be measured alone, as it will be directly related to the other two parts of the formula. If my issues are so severe and run so deeply, as many do, sometimes even going back two or three generations, a desire to change will not be easily seen in me. Any desire to change or lack thereof that I may have will be encouraged or discouraged by my access or lack of access to the resources needed to make the change. In other words, even when I want to change, my situation may lead me to believe change is not possible.

I know a young lady from one of my programs who wanted to go to college. Although she was a poor student in high school, we took her on a college tour anyway. While on that tour, she saw possibilities she previously did not know were available to her. As we saw the impact the college tour had with the female student in the section on exposure, the light bulb went off for this student as well during a college tour, causing her to realize that a better life was possible. She began to get excited about the possibility of creating a better life for herself. She told us that she was going to focus on school more so that she could have a chance at going to college, and I believed her. I could see the gleam in her eyes when she talked about it.

However, when we got home, reality set in, and she was placed back in her old familiar environment, where she began to operate out of her old, familiar mindset. Her previous mindset, being developed from the reality that out of five older siblings, not one had even graduated high school. Out of four older female siblings, all of them were mothers before their 21st birthday, and none of them were married". Alcohol and drugs were as common as food and water, nothing was off limits in the house, and anything was capable of happening at any given moment. The house had been shot up on one occasion, and broken into and robbed on another, all in the six months this student was in the program. So, even though we spent a lot of resources on her; we knew how deeply her issues were, and tried to get her help, we were largely unsuccessful on the surface as she ended up getting pregnant at 19 and never made it to college. Nevertheless, we still could not allow ourselves to feel as though we had somehow failed her. When we look at her story holistically, we did not see her lack of progress as her lacking the desire to change, as much as we saw it as a testament to the depths of her issues.

This young lady was also a survivor of molestation. She said she told her mother about the abuse, but her mother did not do anything about it. When I met the mother I noticed several things that were disturbing. I discovered the mother had a drinking problem, which I confirmed through the daughter who told me that her mother usually started drinking by 8:30 in the morning. The student said that the mother got chronic headaches that were very bad and she drank because the alcohol made her feel better. I also discovered that the mother while strong and confident in her home, acted weak and fragile while we were out, failing to ever look me in the eyes during our interaction. All of these things led me to believe that the mother was probably also a survivor of sexual abuse. I never asked the mother about the abuse because we never developed that kind of relationship.

Another one of my students, a 15 year old young man who recently has dropped out of school as he faces numerous judicial charges is another example. This young man, who stands approximately five feet tall and weighs probably 95 pounds feels as though he is in the world by himself. He has never met his biological mother, and like many children in his g/eneration, does not know his biological father. He has younger half-brothers and sisters, and he lives with the grandmother of some of his younger siblings. His mother is strung out on crack, and left him at birth, which is why he has never met her. The siblings' father is also strung out on crack, but functioned well enough to take his children to his mother's house for her to see about them. This is how our student ended up with his siblings' grandparents. While it seems really noble of them to take a child with whom they have no biological connection, the truth of the matter is that their motives in doing so were not entirely pure. In fact the young man would tell anyone who asked that they kept him because of the check they got for him. The young man had been in their custody since he was two years old. The grandmother is sick with cancer and has neither the will, nor the time to really spend with this young man. In fact, the grandmother has gone as far as to blame this young man for her sickness. She has had him arrested on more than one occasion. She neglects him, as she buys clothes, shoes and other essentials for his siblings without buying anything for him. On one occasion, he showed up to our office with bruises on his face, and plugs of hair cut out of his head. When I asked him what happened, he told me that his uncles had jumped on him because he complained about being the only one to do dishes in the house. When I told him I was mandated to call the Illinois Department of Children and Family Services to report this as abuse he told me to do so. He assured me that: DCFS would investigate; his foster mother would show them his background information; they would be convinced that he was a liar, and nothing would be done. Sure enough, he was absolutely correct. When we made the call, what he said would happen was precisely what happened. The purpose of this work is not to point fingers at any school, individual, or agency, however, the reality is when one looks at the number of DCFS complaints that are listed as unfounded questions should at least be raised about the investigative process.

Anyway, I asked this young man why he thought the grandmother kept him in the house if she did not really care about him. Without hesitation he responded, because she gets a check for me. I began to believe that this feeling of being unwanted was at the root of this young man's problems in school, at home, and his numerous involvements within the judicial system. His self-esteem was non-existent. We tried our best to help him. We provided him with an internship to put money in his pocket to hopefully begin to re-build his broken self-image. We took him shopping. We took him to the barber. We took him to a couple of nice restaurants, just hoping that he would begin to feel better about himself. It seemed to be working. He was smiling more. He was clean, and he maintained a nice haircut. He was doing well. However, we were thrown for a loop when all of a sudden he stopped coming around. He stopped going to school, and we were even more surprised when we found out that he had not been coming home at night either. So, we went looking for him, just sort of driving around the neighborhood searching his hang out spots. After about a month or so, we found him. He looked a mess again, yet he agreed to come to the office to talk with me about what was going on in his life.

As we sat in my office and talked, I could tell that he felt the weight of the world on his shoulders. I could tell because it was a feeling I had felt all too often. He told me that he had been living in an abandoned van and taking showers at a friend's house when the opportunity presented itself. I asked him why he would not go home, and he told me that he did not have a home. I asked him why he would not go back to his foster home, and he told me that he would rather live in the street. The more I talked to him the sorrier I felt for him. There was a point in the conversation where I needed to walk away and regain my composure. This happens quite frequently actually when you work closely with youth and get more and more involved in their personal lives. As we continued to talk and I continued to try and convince him to let us try and help he became more and more despondent. I told him to give us a chance, and he told me that I was wasting my time with him. He said words that I will never forget, "you may as well try and help someone else. I have known since I was four years old that my life was not going to amount to anything." This was when the light bulb went off for me. I realized at that moment that this young man was battling issues that went far deeper than I had imagined. Clean him up, put him in a few workshops, and give him a few dollars and he will be fine I thought. Clearly I had underestimated the depths of his issues.

Because this young man was so gifted in his ability as a writer, it was easy to misdiagnose the depths of his issues. In fact, the judge actually had compassion on him after hearing his work, and said to him on more than one occasion, "I want to help you." We eventually were able to get the judge to order him out of that foster home, assigned to a group home, and registered into sessions with a therapist that he desperately needed. However, eventually he ran away from the group home. His lack of self-esteem, fractured ego, and feelings of being unwanted, all of which had been constantly reinforced from the time he was an infant, proved to be too much to overcome in the year that he was in the program. Despite our many efforts we were not able to locate him again.

With both of these two young people there were multiple layers of issues that had been developed over generations within their family that were impacting these children's desire to change. Once I discovered this, I had to remember it when working with the children. I had to understand, and continue to remind myself that these student had issues that were created over multiple generations that I could not believe would be resolved in the short time they would be in my program. So when confronted with students whose issues are affecting their desire to change, my focus would have to shift from helping them change to helping create in them a desire to change.

In order to create the desire to change that I want to see in my students, my willingness to recognize the students' issues have to transcend normal parameters. One of my students smoked a (marijuana) blunt in the front of our office. Someone saw her and of course came and told me. I confronted the student, and she admitted to smoking the blunt in the front of the office. Instead of kicking her out of the program, or berating her for doing it, I talked to her about how something like that could get the program shut down. She did not stop coming to the program high, but the next time she smoked she went around the corner, and I praised her for doing that. Eventually she started smoking before she came to the program altogether. While the ideal for many would be that she stopped smoking altogether, which we certainly had discussed. I realized at the moment quitting was not a realistic option for her. So rather than push her away by constant conversations regarding her need to quit, I chose to see her progress as a desire to change. When the issues run deep the desire to change will be impacted. When this happens, my tolerance has to be raised, as well as my willingness to continue to invest resources. Otherwise, the students who need help the most will probably never get the help they need.

Access to Resources

Access to Resources will be the single greatest determining factor in your ability to help the youth who are most "troubled". You will find that the young people who are most at risk and need your help the most will require a lot of time, money, and connections to address the issues going on in their lives. Because resources are scarce you will have to be creative and persistent in your efforts to obtain them for your youth. Here are some things you should do:

Be a Community Connector

In order to maximize the amount of support you can get for your youth you will need to familiarize yourself with every social service agency and youth serving program in the area. This will allow you to create a network of providers that you can put in a binder and have available as circumstances arise. If a student tells you that he is homeless you will already have a list of homeless shelters available. If a student tells you they are struggling in math, you will already have a list of agencies that provide free tutoring in math. If you have a student who does not have a coat you will already have a list of places that provide free or cheap coats to needy families. Creating a list of the various services in the community and becoming a community connector will help you and your student in a number of ways:

First and foremost, being a connector with an active list of services available gets your young person the help they need as quickly as possible. If a student is coming to you, it is an emergency and they probably have no place else to go. So you want to be prepared to treat it as an emergency, and the best way to do that is by getting them the help they need as quickly as possible.

The second thing being a connector does is helps to further establish the relationship between you and the student. When a student knows that they can come to you when they need help and you will not only be there for them, but actually get them the help they need, they will begin to trust you more and your ability to help them will increase dramatically.

Being a community connector also helps because it reduces your stress levels as you no longer feel as though you have to personally solve all of the students' problems. When you begin to hear some of your students' stories you will want to do all you can to help them. However, even though the desire to help may be strong, the skill set in some areas may not be. A prime example of this is in the case where one of our mentors asked to be replaced from working with the young lady who suffered from bi-polar disorder. The young lady asking to be replaced was one of our best mentors who cared for the children and had a strong desire to help them. The desire to help can be strong and that is a good thing, but the desire to help coupled with a network of providers who can help is even better.

Finally, being a community connector helps you conserve your own organization's resources. You may have a student who needs transportation to get to and from school. Your organization may have a budget for transportation. However, wouldn't it be nice to know if the school had a budget for transportation for students? The organization could then refer the student to the school to get the help they need; while saving the money in its transportation budget for another student, or maybe to send students on job interviews, or even take students on field trips. Being a community connector allows you to be a good steward over your own limited resources.

Use your friends

One of the things I learned when I was a Club Director responsible for raising hundreds of thousands of dollars annually was that the number one reason people give to support a cause is they believe in the cause. However, the second greatest reason people give to support a cause is because they believe in the person supporting the cause. This is the very reason why charities get celebrities to endorse them, because even if you do not care about the charity you may still give because you care about the celebrity supporting the charity. Denzel Washington is a great example of this. He is a national spokesperson for Boys & Girls Clubs. However he is also recognized as a magnificent actor, and highly regarded as a good father, husband, and positive representation of manhood. When he speaks about his experience growing up in a Boys & Girls Club it is very powerful and resonates with people. Because of who he is, even if people know nothing about Boys & Girls Clubs they will be inclined to give because Denzel Washington is promoting them.

Likewise, the friends who know you well know how much you care about the kids you mentor, and they would be willing to support you in a number of ways.

Donations: This is obviously the best way to get the support of your friends. Even the friends who do not have a lot of money can make small donations to support things you are doing. For example, if you want to have a holiday party and need snacks or drinks, your friends would probably be willing to make small donations to help you with some of the things you need for the party. These small donations will help you provide quality activities for your young people, and keep you from overspending your own money for things.

Company Support: If you have friends who work for major companies, find out if those companies have programs that can help you. Find out where your friends work and do the research to find out what kind of support you can get from the companies your friends work for. I have a friend who worked for JP Morgan Chase. At the time she worked there, Chase had a program where they would donate $1000 to support a one day event that one of its employees was supporting. When I found about this program, Hurricane Katrina had just devastated New Orleans. I put together an event to collect first aid items to put together bags to send to the hurricane survivors. We promoted the event among our parents and students, and collected items for three weeks. We collected miniature first aid kits, wipes, pampers, personal hygiene items and bottled waters. At the end of three weeks we had tons of items. We had my friend from Chase and some of her colleagues come in and work with some of our students to put the bags together (one day event). We found another charity (Operation PUSH in Chicago) that was shipping items to New Orleans and dropped all of our items off on Operation PUSH's designated drop off day. In using my friend's work contact we were able to: contribute much needed support to the survivors of Hurricane Katrina; increase the self-esteem of our students as they learned the value in helping others; and raise an additional $1000 in support for our program in the process. Also, when researching the companies your friends work for check to see if those companies have a matching gifts fund. A lot of companies will match the charitable donations of its employees, doubling any potential gifts your friends may give.

The Three T's

Treasure: Monetary donations again are easily the best way for you to get the support of friends who believe in the work you are doing.

Talent: You may have friends who do not have a lot of money but still want to support you and your efforts. Find out what they are good at and ask them to run a program in the area that interests them. Chances are good that whatever your friend is interested in you will have youth that share that interest. There was one year, during the heart of the recession when fundraising was down and we had to make tremendous cuts. Things were so bad at one point that staffing cuts forced us to limit the number of children we allowed in the building to avoid the danger of violating the state's staff to children ratio. I asked my wife to run a program. She is a graphic designer who creates some of the most beautiful invitations I have ever seen. She agreed to come in once a week to teach a class on graphic design, and I agreed to keep the numbers of the class small. She ended up running an excellent 8 week program, and had 11 girls who followed her around the entire summer. The use of her talent benefited the kids who participated in her program and saved me money in my budget as that was one less program I had to pay for someone to facilitate.

Time: Willingness to work directly with the youth requires a degree of patience that some of your friends may not have. For those who want to help, but are not comfortable working directly with any number of youth, no matter how small the numbers, get them to donate their time. If you can get help for even one hour per week from 3 or 4 friends, it will save you money in your budget and will increase the effectiveness of your program. The more positive adults you can expose your children to the better. The mere presence of these adults in the building benefits the program. However, when you know they are coming find out their strengths and design their volunteer efforts around their strengths so that you maximize the use of their time. Doing so will make your friends feel like they are a part of the program and will increase the likeliness of them staying involved. Some suggestions for volunteer efforts can include:

- ➤ Filing
- ➤ Book keeping
- ➤ Coaching
- ➤ Officiating sporting events
- ➤ Maintenance
- ➤ One-on-one Mentoring
- ➤ Tutoring
- ➤ Facilitating programs
- ➤ Chaperones
- ➤ Special events

Grants

Grants are what I consider a necessary evil in the world of mentoring and youth development. They are necessary in that it is difficult to run a successful program without them. They can be evil because you can fall into the trap of fulfilling the grant requirements at the expense of your students. Some grant requirements can also be very demanding with an award amount inconsistent with the efforts needed to meet the requirements. Here are a few things to remember when looking for grants to subsidize your mentoring program:

Do the research: Make sure you read the grant announcement and RFP (Request for Proposal) thoroughly. Find out which agencies have been funded through that grant in the past. Once you have determined the types of agencies and programs that have been funded in the past, look for similarities in your program that you can emphasize when writing your proposal.

Be selective: Thorough research will also save you time as you can rule out grants that are not a good match for what you are doing. You want to be very selective when choosing grants. Ideally you want to find grants that are looking to fund programs similar to what you are already running. This will minimize the amount of extra work you have to do as you can keep your program as is. You can write off percentages of staff salaries, supply needs, and in some cases even utility costs to run programs that you are already running. Intramural sports tournaments are a good example of this. You may find a grant that wants to address the obesity crisis among America's youth. If you have an intramural sports tournament that you are already running, you can keep that program, add a few health workshops, and meet the requirements for the grant, creating revenue without adding work or changing any other part of your program.

Be prepared: I talked extensively about the importance of paperwork in the chapter on documentation. Grants are an area that stress this importance. Some grantors will want to see your files a couple of times per year. Some may never want to see them. Some grantors will want to have random audits, and some will give you several weeks advance notice that they are coming. The bottom line for you is the best way to serve your students is by being prepared. DO YOUR PAPERWORK.

Go the extra mile: When it comes to grants, most will have some metrics for reporting. Go the extra mile when submitting your reports. Depending on the kind of grant, reporting requirements may include things like: number of students (unduplicated) served, number of students served daily, gender breakdown of participants, and racial and economic demographics served. Program information will want to see the types of programs students participated in, the objectives of those programs, and the outcomes that were achieved through the program. When submitting your report go the extra mile by including:

Pictures: "A picture is worth a thousand words" the old saying goes. As your donor reads your report, any visual images that you have to support what the donor is reading will only enhance your written report by bringing to life the children being helped through the grant.

Personal stories: When appropriate and without being exploitive of your kids, share success stories with your donors. People can relate to stories, and everyone loves a success story. If you have a kid who lost 50 lbs. from participating in an obesity program, share that success (with before and after pictures) with your grantor. The stories, especially when submitted with pictures encourage the grantor to continue giving as they allow the donor to actually see their money at work.

Narrative report: Always include a narrative when submitting your report, even when the report does not require one. Narratives allow you to tell the part of the story that you want emphasized. As I stated in the section on case notes, narratives allow you to speak about program benefits not being looked at in the numbers.

Obstacles: As noble as your efforts may be, getting the amount of resources you will need to truly provide the kind of help your students require will be challenging, presenting you with a couple of obstacles for which you should be prepared.

1. **Obtaining student documents**: When you find yourself attempting to help a student obtain social services or employment services obtaining the necessary documents in a timely manner may become a major obstacle. You will find some parents who are unwilling to provide you with the documents in fear that you will affect the services they may be already getting. You will have some parents who are unable to find the documents

when you need them. Even a task as simple as helping a student with a financial aid application can be a problem as parents may be unwilling to provide the student with the tax documents they need to complete the application. You will do yourself a tremendous favor by creating a list of documents that you request from every student as they sign up for the program. Parents are much more willing to share these documents when they are requested at a non-threatening time.

- Picture ID (High School ID card is usually okay)
- Birth Certificate
- Social Security Card
- Insurance Card (If applicable)
- Application with 2 Emergency Contacts
- Consent Forms

Having these documents on hand will help you be prepared to help your students when situations arise.

2. **The system takes time**: When it comes to the acquisition of resources, remember the system takes time to work. Whether you are waiting to hear if you received a grant for which you have applied, or waiting to see if one of your students was hired for a job he applied, you will always find yourself waiting. This waiting game presents an obstacle. As we have already discussed your ability to make an impact will be defined by your ability to resolve issues presented quickly and satisfactorily. Maintain an emergency fund when possible to help you get immediate assistance as

needed. Even if the emergency fund is small remember in a crisis every little bit helps.

Keep resources close: Try and get lines of credit to help you when cash flow is slow. Use your resources wisely, conserve whenever you can. Your ability to survive burnout and make the kind of impact you hope to make with your students will be directly related to your understanding of your students' issues and your ability to connect them to the resources needed to address those issues. This will require you to be a good steward over the resources you have.

I was recently chatting with some friends on one of the social networking sites about the violence going on in Chicago where so many kids continue to be killed. Suggestions were made about what should be done to address the issue of violence with one person suggesting building more prisons. This person went on to suggest that laws should be changed so that criminals are incarcerated without discussion of parole. My questions to that discussion are the same ones I will pose here. Is there a solution for hopelessness? If there is a solution for hopelessness, can that solution be legislated? The battle we face in attempting to mentor this generation, even more than the guns is the reality that we are battling feelings of hopelessness. If I am a kid who thinks college is not a real answer for me, and I have been told that I am not that smart, and everybody from my family who I know has been born and died in the ghetto. What can you say that will realistically change my opinion of myself? Like the young man who told me that he knew at four years old that he would never amount to anything, many of our other "troubled" youth have internalized this belief as well. Even if they cannot articulate their hopelessness as well as he did, they certainly feel it just as intensely.

Maslow on his hierarchy of needs identified that if physiological/basic needs like food and water are not being met, it is next to impossible to create feelings of safety and stability. If stability is not present, ideas of love and the sense of belonging that love creates cannot be obtained. If love is not felt, then the development of self-esteem will not be possible. When self-esteem is not present, the opportunity for people to recognize the inner-talents that may change their conditions are impossible. Maslow was not writing or researching "troubled" youth when he created his hierarchy of needs, but was actually discussing a theory of human motivation. Yet he points out some very important points that must be considered when working with "troubled" youth.

Children coming from environments where they do not eat everyday are easily susceptible to becoming drug dealers as they get older. In fact they will see nothing wrong with selling drugs because they will equate the sale of drugs with their basic needs being met. Children who come from unstable home lives will join gangs because in the gangs they will find the sense of belonging missing from their home lives. The gang members will become like family, providing children with the love and acceptance they were missing. Children who have not experienced love will have damaged and fractured self-esteem and will find no problem seeing murder as a viable solution. In fact, in an ironic twist of fate, some *children* may see murder as the only solution to obtain the respect they long for.

If we really want to stop the killing of our children we must acknowledge and deal with the depths of the issues causing the killings. A child, regardless of how "troubled" he may be does not pick up a gun until all other avenues have been exhausted. If we are serious in our desire to have them put down the guns, we have to have honest conversations with them to help us identify the reasons they picked the guns up in the first place. Once we have identified the deeper issues, resources must be allocated to address the issues that are identified. A desire to change can then be fostered in youth through exposing them to new ideas and teaching them new ways to live.

The formula for success is actually rather simple. Young people need:

- Mentors who care about and advocate for them.
- Mentors who are available.
- Mentors who are trained in recognizing symptoms of mental health disorders.
- Mentors who are resourceful.
- On-going contact with caring adults willing to volunteer their time.
- Access to resources, including: mental health evaluations and treatment, job training programs, and life classes that teach concepts of self-realization.

- Trade schools and other programs that identify and train them in their natural talents.
- Internships that pay money, and teach self-sufficiency.

When this formula is utilized success will follow. The children, no matter how "troubled" they are will respond to genuine love. Like all other living organisms, when children are fed, loved, nurtured, and given purpose, they too will blossom. Consider the Lotus flower, and its opening petals symbolizing in Buddhism the potential for the soul to expand and blossom into beauty and divinity. Often, when observing the beauty of the lotus we forget that its origins were rooted in mud. Yet in spite of its muddy origins, it understands its purpose and it blooms. When children are loved, nurtured, and given purpose, they too can blossom, despite how muddy their origins may have been.

Chapter Seven

Allow Them the Opportunity to Change

"We don't have to engage in grand, heroic actions to participate in the process of change. Small acts, when multiplied by millions of people, can transform the world." **Howard Zinn**

All of the discussion about change and why change is difficult to achieve raises a question. With all of the barriers and issues preventing students from changing how and when do we ever expect to see change? This question is fair, but does not come with a simple answer. The thing to remember about change is that it never does come easy. Whether you are trying to change a nation or an individual, the change you hope to see will not happen without patience and hard work. I was reminded of this as I watched President Barack Obama fight for re-election. In spite of his many accomplishments, and the great job I thought he did under very difficult circumstances he still struggled for re-election. He struggled largely because the change he promised could not be accomplished in four years. Because the pain people feel is real, the president lost some of the people who supported him the first time, with some arguing that the president did not keep his promises. However, close examination shows just how untrue that argument is. He passed a national health care bill, ended the war in Iraq and began the process of troop withdrawal to end the war in Afghanistan. He weakened terrorists regimes, saw the nation through a recession, repealed "don't ask don't tell", and turned around the auto industry. All while battling some of the greatest opposition any president has faced in recent history, and all in his first term. Yet people still wanted more. The truth of the matter is even with his accomplishments President Obama cannot effect change alone, a point which he has emphasized since his election. Change takes time and the efforts of many. I am reminded of this truth every time I work with a young person. It is one of the many truths that build my tolerance, and helps me give a kid the opportunity to change.

Some of the truths that helped guide my efforts, and will place you in the best position to allow your young people the opportunity to change are:

Patience is a virtue

The story I told of the young lady who smoked the marijuana blunt in front of my office is just one example of the power of exercising patience. Traditional wisdom would have recommended suspension and in some cases expulsion from the program for what could be regarded as blatant disrespect for the program. However, such a course of action while maybe making life easier for us, would have certainly not been in the student's best interest, and would have prevented the subsequent progress we saw.

Remember the big picture, and use it to increase your tolerance. The issues these students have were not created in six months and they will not be resolved in six months. Many of the students you encounter may require years of love, patience, and understanding to help them uncover their wounds. Stay the course. You will sometimes get frustrated with the student's lack of effort, but don't give up on them. Many of their issues come from the fact that many adults have already given up on them. Give the formula time to work. Parents, even those with good parenting skills, teachers, counselors, and principals all have busy schedules. In the case of school personnel they have sometimes hundreds of other students to handle, they need help. We can help them by being patient and continuously advocating for the students. Remember, typically what is in the best interest of the student is in the best interest of all involved. Use everyday opportunities to talk to all involved parties and build relationships. Remember, these relationships will determine your success. Be patient, relationships are not built overnight.

Recognize your limitations

The tendency for those who really care about the children they work with is to try and solve all of the children's problems. This is an admirable quality and is what makes one effective when working with youth. However, having said that, you have to know when you have given your all. Once you have advocated for a child to the best of your abilities, have exhausted all resources available to you, and yet were still unable to get the outcome you desired, accept your defeat. Talk to the child and explain why you did not get the outcome you desired. Be honest, but careful. You may be able to salvage the relationship, or you may not. The child may understand, but he may not. How the child receives the disappointment is out of your control, but being honest will help you feel better about the disappointment. Allowing yourself to feel guilty will drain you of energy that you will definitely need to help the next student face the next obstacle.

Remember, no matter how well intentioned you are, you cannot save them from their lives. Your own mental health will be a key factor in your ability to make an impact. Take breaks when needed. Outside of major emergencies, which I have always defined as someone bleeding, you do not have to address every issue the moment it occurs. Taking breaks throughout the day will make you much more effective when you do have situations that require your immediate attention.

Less is better

When it comes to mentoring, the rule of thumb I have always followed is less is better. The numbers will likely depend on factors like grant requirements, and budgets. However, an ideal ratio for mentors is 1:5 with 1:10 being the absolute maximum. Anything more than this will limit the effectiveness of the mentors. Each student will require a set amount of individual time to spend with his mentor. The mentor will also need time for group hours. If a mentor has ten students he mentors, and he is scheduled to spend four hours per week with each student, which is less than an hour per day, then one mentor serving ten students will use a forty hour week just spending much needed individual time with his students. Individual time is most important because it is where the relationships are built. However, the forty hour week does not include travel time, paperwork, phone calls and text messages when the students need the mentors' help, group activities that will be necessary to discuss social behaviors, field trips, or team building activities. All of these components are necessary for a successful program.

When grant requirements and budget issues force you to work with less than ideal numbers use your friends and network. You may be forced to assign mentors more students than you are comfortable, if so you can still ensure their effectiveness by giving the mentors less responsibilities. Remember, less is better. Bring in outside consultants to teach classes, friends to help with filing, and any other assistance you can provide that will free time for the mentors to spend more time with their students.

Recognition is essential

In order to get the most from your mentors as well as your students, recognizing their efforts will be most important. You will be asking a lot of your mentors and when they go beyond the call of duty recognizing their efforts will encourage them to continue to give their all. Likewise, you are asking your students in many cases to do things they are not accustomed to doing and when they do so, it will generally be because they have extended themselves to great lengths in order to not let you down.

Recognizing the efforts of your staff and students serves several purposes:

- Recognition motivates staff and students to go beyond the call of duty, and take risks, allowing them to further their own development.
- Recognition builds internal drive and promotes opportunities for self-reflection and growth.
- Recognition encourages individual effort, and builds self-esteem.
- Recognition provides the opportunity to measure achievement over periods of time.

The importance of recognition hit me one day when I came home from work. I came in one night after work and my wife had prepared a wonderful meal. During this time period I was serving as a director so I was earning a decent salary, allowing my wife to stay at home and perform the important task of being a home-maker. So I had grown accustomed to her preparing these wonderful meals. On this particular night, as we sat down to eat my wife said, "You didn't say anything about me cooking dinner tonight." So, after I thanked her for cooking dinner, I thought about what she said and it dawned on me that *everyone* wants to be recognized for what they do, even when they are expected to do it.

The incident with my wife changed my perspective on the importance of recognition, but also on the importance of understanding the worth of people's contribution. Without my wife preparing meals, cleaning, doing laundry, and performing all of the other duties that go with being a home-maker, I would not have had the time, mental focus, or energy to give the students or the staff, the kind of effort they came to expect of me. This realization made me a better manager as I came to truly appreciate and recognize the contributions of everyone. As the director, my job was to raise money to keep the doors open. However, if the program director did not run a quality program schedule, the kids would not want to come, and I could not raise money without kids to serve. If the program staff did not make the programs fun and engaging, the kids would not come and I would not be able to raise money. If the janitor did not keep the building clean, potential donors would be less likely to give because people are less inclined to contribute resources to an organization that is not taking care of the resources that it currently has. The lesson is that everyone's role is important and everyone wants and deserves to be recognized. Mentors will work long and hard hours to develop the kind of relationships that will allow you to help your students. The students will make extraordinary efforts, sometimes against great obstacles to help you in your efforts to help them. Find ways to both formally and informally acknowledge their efforts.

Informal recognition should occur for both staff and children on a continual basis. Mentioning special efforts made by staff and students during staff meetings and assemblies is one way of recognition. Movie passes, gift cards, bus cards, gas cards, and gift certificates provide a variety of rewards that can be used as part of recognition efforts. Certificates of achievement, student/mentor of the month awards, pizza parties, and even certificates of participation are all excellent tools to recognize the efforts of students and mentors. Include regular recognition ceremonies as part of the planned program, but make time to recognize efforts on a consistent basis as well.

When all else fails

When all else fails, and you have exhausted every ounce of energy on a kid, act in the most loving way possible. Rather real or perceived, many of the youth you will identify as "troubled" will be "troubled" primarily because they feel unloved. You can make a tremendous impact by just being there. Even when you cannot change their circumstances, you can always show some love. A little bit of love goes a long, long way. If you do not believe it I have a challenge for you. The next time you are having a bad day, or feeling down, call someone you KNOW loves you and tell them you are feeling down. This person may be a friend, a parent, or a sibling. The only criteria is that you and this person truly love each other. If possible schedule a time to go by and see that person. The challenge is to either get a hug from that person, or tell them you need to know they love you. By the time you leave their presence I guarantee you will feel better. Your problem will not be gone, but you will feel better because a little bit of love goes a long, long way.

Remember that your students are no different than you, and you are the one whom they will call when they need a hug or a kind word. Oftentimes your presence in their lives is enough. Be there for them. Even the students you may not get in time to truly help, be there for them while you can. The love you show them while you have them will be with them long after they leave your program. I heard a story that provides a perfect illustration of this point.

One day a man was walking along the beach, picking up starfish and throwing them back out into the ocean. The man seemed oblivious to anything else except the starfish. Another man, sitting there on the beach, watched the entire thing. One after another the man picked up the starfish and took his time and threw each one he picked up as far out into the ocean as he could. Finally, the man reached the stranger who sat and watched him. When the stranger spoke to him, he never took his eyes off the starfish. "Why are you doing this?" The stranger asked. "It is not like what you are doing is really making a difference. There are millions of starfish on the beach, so the few you are throwing out into the ocean is not making a difference. Your hard work and commitment means nothing. So, I ask you again, why are you doing this?" The man, while still throwing starfish, and without looking up said, "To the millions on the beach, it means nothing, but to the ones being thrown back it means everything." For mentors, teachers, counselors, coaches, concerned neighbors, friends, and all others who work with young people, and those who just want to help, the story of the starfish should be our motivation and should set the standard. If this is our standard, and love is the tool by which we hope to reach this standard, then we will reach our children in a powerful way, and *our presence* will *allow them the opportunity to change.*

Notes

"American Academy of Child & Adolescent Psychiatry." *American Academy of Child & Adolescent Psychiatry.* N.p., n.d. Web. 28 May 2013.

"American Foundation for Suicide Prevention." *American Foundation for Suicide Prevention.* N.p., n.d. Web. 28 May 2013.

Ellison, Ralph. *Invisible Man.* New York: Vintage International, 1995. Print.

Fanon, Frantz. *The Wretched of the Earth.* New York: Grove, 1965. Print.

"Franklin D. Roosevelt: Undelivered Address Prepared for Jefferson Day." *Franklin D. Roosevelt: Undelivered Address Prepared for Jefferson Day.* N.p., n.d. Web. 28 May 2013.

"Governor's Council on Mental Health Stigma | About Us." *Governor's Council on Mental Health Stigma | About Us.* N.p., n.d. Web. 28 May 2013.

"Hierarchy of Needs." *About.com Psychology.* N.p., n.d. Web. 28 May 2013.

"Howard Zinn: Small Acts Multiplied by Millions." *National Catholic Reporter.* N.p., n.d. Web. 28 May 2013.

Kiyosaki, Robert T., and Sharon L. Lechter. *Rich Dad, Poor Dad: What the Rich Teach Their Kids about Money-- That the Poor and Middle Class Do Not!* New York: Warner Business, 2000. Print.

Life After Hate. N.p., n.d. Web. 28 May 2013.

"Margaret Mead Quotes." *Margaret Mead Quotes (Author of Coming of Age in Samoa).* N.p., n.d. Web. 28 May 2013.

"The Myth Of The Cave By Plato." *The Myth Of The Cave By Plato.* N.p., n.d. Web. 28 May 2013.

"NIMH · Home." *NIMH RSS.* N.p., n.d. Web. 28 May 2013.

O'Neal, Tatum. *A Paper Life.* New York: Harper Entertainment, 2004. Print.

Parsloe, Eric, and Monika Jamieson. Wray. *Coaching and Mentoring: Practical Methods to Improve Learning.* London: Kogan Page, 2000. Print.

"Sandra Day O`Connor Quotes." *Sandra Day O`Connor Quotes.* N.p., n.d. Web. 28 May 2013.

Woodson, Carter Godwin. *The Mis-education of the Negro.* Chicago, IL: African-American Images, 2000. Print.

About the Author

Sidney W. Johnson was born and raised on the south side of Chicago. He attended Northern Illinois University where he studied English and African American studies. While a student at NIU Sidney worked for Project Upward Bound where he discovered a passion for working with young people. Awarded the Etiquette Foundation of Illinois' Humanitarian Award in 2011 for his efforts to empower youth Sidney has dedicated his career to that cause. For the past 18 years Sidney has worked in some of the toughest neighborhoods in Chicago. From Abla Homes where he rebuilt a state funded program to award winning status, to East Garfield Park, where he revived a struggling board to help keep a facility open for youth, to Roseland where he built a mentoring program that helped high risk students see improvements in grade point average, and attendance while seeing a decrease in out of school suspensions and behavioral related incidents. Sidney's passion for working with young people has taken him all over the country training youth workers on Developing Positive Relationships with Youth and Effective Guidance and Discipline.

www.ingramcontent.com/pod-product-compliance
Lightning Source LLC
Chambersburg PA
CBHW072241270326
41930CB00010B/2221